Missing Persons

THE AARON WILDAVSKY FORUM
FOR PUBLIC POLICY

Edited by Lee Friedman

This series is to sustain the intellectual excitement that Aaron Wildavsky created for scholars of public policy everywhere. The ideas in each volume are initially presented and discussed at a public lecture and forum held at the University of California.

Aaron Wildavsky, 1930–1993

"Your prolific pen has brought real politics to the study of budgeting, to the analysis of myriad public policies, and to the discovery of the values underlying the political cultures by which peoples live. You have improved every institution with which you have been associated, notably Berkeley's Graduate School of Public Policy, which as Founding Dean you quickened with your restless innovative energy. Advocate of freedom, mentor to policy analysts everywhere."

*(Yale University, May 1993, from text granting
the honorary degree of Doctor of Social Science)*

1. *Missing Persons: A Critique of the Social Sciences,* by Mary Douglas and Steven Ney

Missing Persons

A Critique of the Social Sciences

Mary Douglas and Steven Ney

UNIVERSITY OF CALIFORNIA PRESS

Berkeley   Los Angeles   London

RUSSELL SAGE FOUNDATION

New York

University of California Press
Berkeley and Los Angeles, California

University of California Press, Ltd.
London, England

These figures and tables were previously published: fig. 1—
George du Maurier, *Punch* 79 (Oct. 30), 1880, p. 194; figs. 4
and 7—Christian Brunner, in Serge Prêtre, *Nucléaire symbol-
isme et société: Contagion mentale ou conscience des risques?*,
SFEN, Paris, 1989, pp. 8–9, 13; fig. 6—Karl Dake, "The
Meanings of Sustainable Development: Household Strate-
gies for Managing Needs and Resources," in Scott D.
Wright, ed., *Human Ecology: Crossing Boundaries*, Society for
Human Ecology, Fort Collins, Colo., 1993, p. 431; table 2—
Drewnowski and Scott 1996 (cited in R. Erikson, *The Scan-
dinavian Model: Welfare States and Welfare Research*, M. E.
Sharpe, Armonk, N.Y., 1987, pp. 180–81; table 3—*Human
Development Report*, United Nations Development Pro-
gramme, 1991, pp. 24–25; table 4—Robert Putnam, *Making
Democracy Work: Civic Traditions in Modern Italy*, Princeton
University Press, 1993, p. 31.

Library of Congress Cataloging-in-Publication Data

Douglas, Mary.
    Missing persons : a critique of the social sciences / Mary
Douglas and Steven Ney.
        p. cm.
    Includes bibliographical references and index.
    ISBN 0-520-20752-1 (alk. paper)
        1. Poverty—History.   2. Poor.   3. Social sciences—
Philosophy.   4. Welfare economics.
I. Ney, Steven.   II. Title.
HC79.P6D677   1998
    362.5—dc21   98-12747

Printed in the United States of America
9 8 7 6 5 4 3 2 1

Dedicated to the Memory of Aaron Wildavsky

THE AARON WILDAVSKY
DISTINGUISHED LECTURES
IN PUBLIC POLICY

It is with great pleasure that we inaugurate this series in honor of Aaron Wildavsky (1930–1993). Aaron was one of the giants of twentieth-century political science. As the Founding Dean of the Graduate School of Public Policy at the University of California, Berkeley, he was present at the creation of, and contributed vitally to, the inchoate field of public policy. His written works reflected his enormous range of interests, and included seminal contributions to the study of budgeting, policy analysis, the presidency, and political culture and risk management. Aaron's collegiality and organizational talents matched his prolific pen. He fostered a lively intellectual community wherever he went, whether spending years shaping a new school, or chairing a department, or delivering a host of guest lectures. He reached across disciplinary boundaries, for he appreciated that no single discipline has a monopoly on insights important for improving public policy.

With this lecture series, we seek to honor Aaron's many and vital contributions. We hope that the series will be a means of continuing the intellectual excitement that Aaron brought to so many. The series will involve scholars from diverse disciplines and perspectives, invited by the University of California Wildavsky Forum Committee, who have the common interest of wanting to bring social science to bear on public policy issues.

As series editor, it is my pleasure to thank all the individuals and institutions who have helped to launch this series. I am grateful to the many friends, colleagues, and former students of Aaron, to the Russell Sage Foundation, the Hewlett Foundation, and others for the generous financial support that has helped create the Wildavsky Forum for Public Policy. I am grateful, as well, to James H. Clark and Eric Wanner for their support and assistance in arranging for the publication of this series jointly by the University of California Press and the Russell Sage Foundation.

Most especially, I would like to thank Mary Douglas and Steven Ney for their graciousness in rearranging long-planned scholarly activities to accommodate the timing and intellectual demands of this series. I am confident that this resulting inaugural volume is one that Aaron Wildavsky would have been proud of inspiring.

Lee S. Friedman
Series Editor

CONTENTS

List of Figures and Tables   xi

Preface   xiii

1. Absent Persons in the Social Sciences

   1

2. The Strong Presence of *Homo Œconomicus*

   22

3. Communication Needs of Social Beings

   46

4. For a Concept of the Whole Person

   74

5. Four Whole Persons

   96

6. Persons in the Policy Process

   117

7. The Adversarial Mode

135

8. Shackled by Institutions

154

9. *Homo Œconomicus:* A Way of Saying Nothing

174

Bibliography 187

Index 205

FIGURES AND TABLES

FIGURES

1. "The Six-Mark Teapot"   55
2. The solar modem   57
3. The cultural map   101
4. Swiss commentary on cultural theory   105
5. Four selves in four cultures   109
6. Household cultures and self-reported behavior   111
7. The dialogue of the deaf   142

TABLES

1. Four Conversations about Human Needs and Wants   6
2. Self-Actualization   50

3. The Human Development Index for Individual
Countries 65

4. The Depolarization of Regional Councilors
in Italy 132

PREFACE

This essay by an anthropologist and a political scientist is in homage to Aaron Wildavsky. In his honor the argument can be polemical, for he was polemical, but it must not be negative. Though he was sharp in criticism, farsighted in spotting policy problems, and quick to see a dead-end or a blocked path long before it became apparent to others, he was always fertile in solutions. So it behooves us to be constructive.

We chose the topic to interest the Graduate School for Public Policy at the University of California, Berkeley, hoping to make a combined approach to the social science discourse on poverty and welfare. But we were defeated by what always obstructs anthropologists who try to train their gaze on contemporary local issues. Rebellious parallels from other places will not be subdued; unacceptable comparisons and unlikely conclusions suggest themselves. Overwhelmed by paradox we try turning the microscope around, in order to see the details from some more distant vantage point. But it is impossible. The modes of thought are utterly different. The ideas we have in England, Germany, France, Italy, and the United States about poverty have been accommodated to paradox by centuries of use. This is what usage does to contradiction. Consequently, this exercise has to be devoted to finding common ground. The assumptions of the social sciences must be expanded to meet ideas from other cultures. We are obliged to retreat from identifying symptoms of poverty and the perversity of local policies: The microscope itself must be our subject. The social sciences are an apparatus for seeing, and we must mark the areas that have been occluded by the equipment. Several dark places show up, but the most extensive is the idea of the person to whose impoverishment or welfare the theorizing attends. Consequently, this has become not a discussion of poverty, though that topic was the impetus for the rest of our consideration, but a discussion of a blind spot that has frequently been noted before, especially by anthropologists. It is the defective theory of the person, how the defects came about, and why they are so difficult to remedy. These are admittedly rather well-worn topics, and to honor Aaron's originality we also feel bound to be constructive. Thus we have tried to expose a theory of the person that underlies the cultural theory to which his work contributed so much.

CHAPTER ONE

Absent Persons
in the Social Sciences

ANTHROPOLOGISTS' CONUNDRUMS
ABOUT POVERTY

Anthropologists observe people over the globe who lack beds, cupboards, houses, and most of the conventional materials of physical comfort, but they may not necessarily be counted poor, and they often do not count themselves as such. The social sciences describe poverty as a material lack, as the converse of possessing wealth. By definition a poor person is without material means. This implies that if these means could be supplied, the poverty would be cured and well-being assured. The materialist bias is part of a historical legacy, an ancient political responsibility for ensuring that citizens have roofs over their heads, larders with food to eat, and beds to sleep in.

A favorite idea among those who deal with poverty professionally is that the high technology of advanced capitalism supplies these lacking things and, in addition, nurtures the political conditions for their enjoyment. Their absence (that is, poverty) in various noncapitalist countries was used as a defense of capitalism. But in the 1960s, when political complacency was challenged, this confidence also started to fade. In the 1980s a critical literature began to douse the fond hopes of philanthropists. On the dustcover of Vic George's book, *Wealth, Poverty and Starvation: An International Perspective*, there is a cartoon of a little man looking at the view from the top of an eminence labeled EEC Food Mountain and saying: "On a clear day you can see Ethiopia"—this at a time when famine gripped that country (George 1988). Programs to feed the hungry of the industrially undeveloped nations would patently bring wealth to the food producers of the developed countries (Griffin 1987; Raikes 1988). Programs to help the undeveloped countries to produce their own food were patently advantageous to exporters of agricultural machinery. As for programs to industrialize the nonindustrial nations, the worthiness of the projects justified ruthless competition to open new markets and to break down subsistence economies (Goodman and Redclift 1991). When there seemed to be no way to do good to others without doing good to oneself, innocence was lost. Altruism became suspect; selfish interest and ideological bias lurked under every pulpit.

Almost simultaneously anthropologists announced two discoveries: Both affluence and freedom were already available without benefit of technology. Consider what the constituent elements of affluence include: short working hours; convivial company; food to eat and to share; social obligations that can be fulfilled; intellectual stimulus; opportunity to reflect on history and mythology, to speculate on metaphysics, to compose poetry and practice rhetoric; time and opportunity for grooming, praying, singing, and dancing together in beautiful surroundings. All these can be had without possessing the material things that mark absence of poverty in the West.

The paradox is old and well known. In the 1960s documentation was collected from herders and the hunting and gathering societies. That pastoralism was a hard life of unremitting vigilance and toil was questioned. Philip Gulliver had already shown how few hours of work are required for an African pastoralist economy (Gulliver 1955). Even less in a hunting economy: A famous time-and-motion study made the demonstration for Australian hunters (McArthur and McCarthy 1960); Woodburn reckoned likewise for Tanzanian savannah hunters (Woodburn 1968). In the Congo equatorial rain forest, Turnbull showed how much leisure time the pygmies disposed of, while the Bantu agriculturalists in the forest clearings worked harder and faced more uncertainty (Turnbull 1961). Marshall Sahlins worked out the main theory of primitive affluence (1968, 1974), which directed attention toward the motives, particularly the political motives, for production. If motivation to accumulate is weak, the wants are simple and can be fulfilled. Relative to perceived physical wants, the Stone Age economy is an economy of abundance.

It is generally agreed that something other than material goods is essential for true affluence to prevail: The good things have to be enjoyed in acceptable democratic freedom. Equity is the other aspect of individual well-being. Here again anthropologists have a message of their own. The rule of law and guarantees of freedom of speech are found in very poor places. The nomadic Guayaki Indians in the tropical forests of Paraguay, without recourse to the ballot box, seem to exemplify Montesquieu's constitutional ideals

(Abensour 1987). And the people who are poorest in material things are often those who display the most resolute commitment to political freedom and equality (Berreman 1981).

From this basis the anthropologists seemed ready in the 1960s or 1970s to launch a critique of the concept of poverty as it is used in the social sciences. But the move stalled. The position turns out to be weak in debate. It is indeed awkward to be implicitly reactionary and yet radical at the same time. How are the hearers supposed to respond? Is the message that we can abolish poverty and establish true democracy if we all set out for a life of herding or hunting? It is provocative to say that the hunter is the reverse of the economic man because "his wants are scarce and his means (in relation) plentiful," but the coda makes clear that Sahlins is attacking the established discourse at a high level of philosophical generality: "We are inclined to think of hunters and gatherers as *poor* because they don't have anything; perhaps better to think of them for that reason as *free*" (Sahlins 1974: 13–14).

That small is beautiful is in itself a seductively beautiful idea, one that keeps rearing its head and producing confusion among political scientists, as we shall see later. At one level the radical conversation needs a different concept of poverty, not blocked by a concept that focuses on an individual's need for goods. At another administrative and political level it has to be about material things—cost of living, telephones, air conditioning, central heating, television, and refrigeration. Marshall Sahlins was clearly not about to tell the industrial poor that they should reduce their wants and that they would be happy and free without welfare handouts. The problems of paradox and contradiction arise when policy debates about local public assistance are escalated to a general theory of poverty. If we are not content with arm waving we must try to reorganize the terms of the discourse.

The idea of poverty combines three ideas. One is lack, the second is asymmetry of possession, and the third is the person who is in poverty. "Poor" is always relative. "Poor" also carries a judgment on distribution; hence it also involves equity. Lacking the means of subsistence is not intrinsic to the idea, because we can be poor without being on the brink of starvation. Over the course of two centuries of public policy in England, the idea of dire poverty has acquired a new meaning: Not just lack but potentially lethal lack, to the point of destitution, means having so little that our physical subsistence is endangered.

The idea we have now of bare subsistence or subsistence level comes from its important role in Ricardo's economic theory and its role in Malthus's population theory expecting that increase of population will always drive laborers' wages below subsistence level and, again, in Marx's theory of the incorporation of labor value into prices. Even if it were not for these issues, subsistence level had to be measured for welfare administration. Measurability of this lowest point of poverty made it a physiological and material matter.

The Anglo-Saxon social thought that was built on these inquiries has burgeoned into at least four separate discourses on poverty and human needs (Table 1). They all have one thing in common: concern with needs of a generalized human individual conceived as nonsocial or presocial. The fragmented conversations, with their different assumptions and terminologies, correspond to the fragmented pattern of responsibilities in which the carefully fenced-off conversations are held. In this system of thought it is as if the subjects, individual selves, are alone with their needs in a world consisting of objects, some of which can satisfy the needs. No one else is there. Or, rather, there is no theorizing about anyone else. This may not seem a handicap to

TABLE I. FOUR CONVERSATIONS
ABOUT HUMAN NEEDS AND WANTS

Nonsocial Individual			
Needs		*Wants*	*Capabilities*
Basic	Higher		
Famine relief, public assistance, welfare agencies	Arts, self-fulfillment, pleasures of altruism	Economist's revealed preferences of individuals	Actualization of individual capabilities, access to opportunities for self-development, equity

others, but to the anthropologist it is utterly disabling. Of course there are really many more than four official conversations about welfare in the context of policy, but most of them are embedded in the relevant institutions for measuring, deciding on, and administering subsistence or for arguing about it.

The four conversations are laid out in Table 1 to illustrate how ideas are wrapped in and protected by and receive their support from the institutions that embed them. They have little interaction with each other, which probably prevents disagreements from flaring up, and they share one assumption. All four analyze poverty as relating to individuals, and the individual is stripped of distracting attributes so that he or she is as far as possible the same as any other individual.

The basic-needs discourse has a strong practical interest in measures of subsistence and physiological levels of survival to be used in administration of relief. Destitution or indigence would be a better term for the part of the poverty syndrome for which it speaks. For these reasons altruism and spiritual joys have been omitted from the list of basic needs.

A more recent approach in this vein is the literature on basic human needs. Human existence, argue theorists such as Katrin Lederer (1980) or Johan Galtung (1990), can be succinctly described by a system of abstract needs such as freedom or security. These abstract systems of needs are supposed to be immune to cultural distortion: They are truly universal human needs. Thus basic-human-needs systems provide a universal and rational basis for policy arguments. As attractive as this claim may be, we have shown elsewhere (Douglas, Gasper, and others 1998) that, in practice, policymakers ignore cultural projections of human needs at their peril. The work on higher needs goes beyond the materialist definitions, a literature largely inspired by the demand for better surveys of opinion.

The wants discourse is conducted by econometricians who study patterns of consumption and distribution of income. It is outside its scope to determine the right bundle of purchases to save the consumer from falling below the level of basic needs. When the buyer takes home the shopping basket, there is no more interest in what happens to its contents than if they were to be consumed on the spot: Needs are individual needs.

The framing context of basic needs, higher needs, and con-sumption theory cannot give foothold for the larger distribu-tional issues or questions about self-development and equity that appear in the fourth column of Table 1 and that are discussed at a high degree of generality. It is entirely proper that the official discourse should make comparisons of welfare and should need to make accurate and objective measurements. It makes perfectly good sense, for fairness's sake, to say nothing of ease of administration, that there has to be standardization and abstraction. Measuring by common standards meets the bureaucratic need to test false claims and to deal consistently with true ones.

However, there is no need for ideas of human beings' welfare to be couched uniquely in terms of the wants of individuals. In welfare economics and in theories of social justice the standardized individual is alone in an unpopulated landscape. Anthropology is divided from the rest of social science on the idea of the human being, and few divisions are more fundamental. It is awkward to have a nonsocial being at the center of the so-called social sciences. There must be consequences from defining a human as a nonsocial being.

How would it help policymaking to have a different definition? If the topic has to do with material inequalities, does it matter how the individual recipient of handouts is defined? As long as there is no unfair or arbitrary discrimination, surely the fragmented conversations about well-being can do no harm? Perhaps not, or perhaps yes: Their being so tightly locked into their institutional environments may be a drawback. The partitions have effect of censorship: Some questions cannot be raised; some ideas cannot even be phrased so as to go across the barriers.

PERSON AS LOCUS OF TRANSACTIONS

Anthropologists perceive some disadvantages in this mode of thought. Marilyn Strathern calls the Western idea of "the free-standing, self-contained individual" a folk model, in which, "because society is likened to an environment . . . it is possible for Euro-Americans to think of individual persons as relating not to other persons but to society as such, and to think of relations as after the fact of the individual's personhood rather than integral to it" (Strathern 1992: 124–125). Strathern goes on to say that an anthropologist would be scandalized at the idea of a nonrelational definition of the person. On this she has no trouble finding testimony from other anthropologists among whom the idea of the person has been a central issue throughout the twentieth century.

Furthermore, anthropologists analyzing the concept of the gift in Melanesia find themselves shackled by the Western concept of altruism because it is based on the distinction between self-interested and other-interested motives. The distinction fouls up interpretation in cultures where the motives of selves are always thought to be other-directed.

When Strathern says, somewhat enigmatically, that for "person" one could write "gift," she is not being flippant. In Melanesia a person is considered the nodal point at which converge various pathways of giving and receiving. For these people it would be possible to sum up personal identity by the network of transactions in which that person has been engaged and can be expected to create in the future. For a biography it is not an outrageous idea. As we shall show, we could make sense of the same concepts in thinking about our own identities if it were not for some curious assumptions we have inherited. To recognize that a main motive for acquiring objects is to be able to give them away is very different from an implicit assumption that consumption goods are acquired to be consumed by the buyer. Here we begin to locate the points where the present social science discourse does not serve well in comparisons of poverty and well-being.

There are several reasons why the contemporary social sciences make the idea of the person stand on its own, without social attributes or moral principles. Emptying the theoretical person of values and emotions is an atheoretical move. We shall see how it is a strategy to avoid threats to objectivity. But in effect it creates an unarticulated space whence theorizing is expelled and there are no words for saying what is going on. No wonder it is difficult for anthropologists to say what they know about other ideas on the nature of persons and other definitions of well-being and poverty. The path of their argument is closed. No one wants to hear about alternative theories of the person, because a theory of persons tends to be heavily prejudiced. It is insulting to be told that your idea about persons is flawed. It is like being told you have misunderstood human beings and morality, too. The context of this argument is always adversarial.

On the other hand, it is virtually impossible to argue successfully for an alternative view of the person. The idea of the person always has moral and political applications. Two examples from anthropology may make that point clearer. In the first an idea of the person is used by an anthropologist to applaud Western civilization and to confound colleagues; in the other the idea is used to subvert both Western civilization and colleagues.

In a minor essay, "Une Catégorie de l'esprit humain: La Notion de personne, celle de 'moi'," Marcel Mauss briefly surveyed a wide range of ethnography and modern and ancient history and separated the idea of a person into *personnage* on the one hand—that is, a set of public roles or masks—and on the other, conscience, identity, and true consciousness (Mauss 1938). He proposed that to have transcended the limited awareness of the role-playing self was a slowly gained historical achievement of

Western civilization. After the Greeks, Christianity made its contribution to developing self-awareness, and, going by Spinoza and Descartes, the evolution culminated in the sophistication of Hume, Berkeley, and Kant. This flattering view was much favored by Renaissance scholars, but it is out of keeping with Mauss's other writings, on the gift, for example, in which he was very critical of modern culture. The point of the argument in Mauss's hands was that he could distinguish two parts of the person: one outside, cruder, more mechanical; one interior, sensitive, and aware. While paying honor to the second of the pair, the innermost, real person, he was able to take a swipe at the fashionable sociological theories of Malinowski and Durkheim.

MYTHIC PARTICIPATIONS

It is tempting to suppose that Mauss wrote this untypical essay under the influence of Maurice Leenhardt, the missionary-ethnographer from New Caledonia. Leenhardt's biographer, James Clifford (1982), says how much Leenhardt found that he had in common with Mauss—surprisingly, for his own view of religion was strongly inclined to the mystical. He did not expect to find sympathy in Mauss, whom he saw as aggressively secular, a scholar whose collaborative writing with Durkheim was reductionist and determinist. But it turned out that the two shared a concern for the irreducible notion of "the person," that both resisted reducing this category either to the individual of the psychologist or to the collectivity of the sociologist.

Leenhardt used the idea of the person not to applaud Western civilization but, quite the contrary, to extol an alternative. This was represented by the "decentered" conception of the person entertained by the New Caledonian Canaque. Mauss had suggested that the early evolutionary stages of culture only saw the external mask and ignored the inarticulate person inside, but the Canaque person gave the lie to Mauss's belief that primitive civilizations have no skill for turning their thoughts reflexively upon themselves. Far from being dominated by formal roles, Canaque self-understanding was developed in participatory states of consciousness, immersed in living myth, new occasions calling forth new strategies. In their thought, interaction with other selves was the context for shifting perceptions among past, present, and mythical no-time, here and elsewhere in space, moving easily between incongruent mystical images (Leenhardt 1947). It sounds a spontaneous, poetical way of reflection, always open to the moment, not overly committed to hard logic, a succession of participatory states of being.

Leenhardt was a charismatic teacher. He was patently using his view of the Canaque as ammunition against his own adversaries—the missionaries, the traders, the colonial government. Any students inclined to be hostile to structure, logic, and system (especially to Descartes) would flock to his banner. Michel Leiris, the surrealist poet who studied with him, felt support for his own hostility to "the abstractions of intellectualist social science." He said that Leenhardt's style of teaching presented a total contrast: The teacher simply tried "to think aloud 'like a Canaque' . . . taking for his main order of business the dense dilemmas of a single ongoing translation project" (Clifford 1982: 157). It must have been a fascinating experience, learning to think like a Canaque. It would be something like listening to a lion speak.

Wittgenstein said that if a lion could talk, we would not be able to understand him (1953: 223). So how did it happen that the students did understand Leenhardt and used the message they received from him to shape their lives? Daniel Dennett explains it thus: "I think, on the contrary, that if a lion could talk that lion would have a mind so different from the general run of lion minds, that although we could understand him just fine we would learn little about ordinary lions from him" (Dennett 1991: 447).

How much Leenhardt's mode of teaching taught students about the way the Canaque people think or about the Canaque idea of the person is also doubtful. But this is not where the real problems lie. If we are to revise the contemporary idea of the person and keep it precise enough for use in the social sciences, there are two difficulties. One is how to discount the political loading; the other is the problem of the glove. No one can toss away his or her regular notion of the person like an old glove and pick up another one and expect it to fit. It is not a matter of habit. Thinking about persons and developing a standard common notion is the result of interactions and shared judgments of what it takes to be a good person, a complete person, the difference between an immature or an adult person, and so on.

In his Durkheimian phase Mauss had shown primitive classification, knowledge of space and time, and bodily techniques to be enmeshed with social experience (Durkheim and Mauss 1903; Mauss 1936, 1950). In his early work under Durkheim's sway there was no question of his presenting these categories as independent ratiocinations. Persons, whether inhabitants of the Australian desert or of Greenland, would be doing their classifying pragmatically in order to organize their life together. Yet when it came later on to writing about the category of the person, Mauss offered a series of idealist formulations. His friend and colleague offered a series of mystical perceptions. Neither is any help to our project, which is grounded in the thinking of Durkheim and Mauss when they wrote *Primitive Classification*. In that tradition the concept of the person is no peripheral decoration; it is a practical box of tools for dealing with others.

If there really are people who live most of the time in a state of mythic participation and if that means that their idea of the person is weakly articulated and inconsistent, then we can assume that they place little value on coordination and perhaps even that they do not need to coordinate very much. Elsewhere the idea of the person is put into a body furnished with attributes fit to serve complex sets of quite precise expectations. African anthropology has many beautifully written examples of how exterior and interior persons are appointed with the furnishings for elaborate forms of social intercourse (Jackson and Karp 1990; Jacobson-Widding 1991).

As for them, so it is for us: The person in action and the person in thought converge in the claims that people allow to be made. The task of the next chapter will be to examine the dominant model of the person in Western culture. When the strong presence of *Homo œconomicus* is explained by the claims of the economy, we will see the need for a simple, nonpolitical, flexible model of the person devised to suit our other theoretical needs. We will also see how closely the idea of the rational individual is connected with the ideal of objectivity.

THE FRAGILE WESTERN CONSENSUS

Every now and again there is a grand cleanup, when current terms are inspected and some are thrown out of the window. It happens because every now and again some shock has exposed intellectual confusion that had been happily tolerated before. Such a shock may happen at any time. All it takes is for bureaucratic barriers to crumble, for academic disciplines to dissolve a little more, or for a new revivalist sect to take people by storm. Whenever once-separated compartments open up, politics breaks in, and the tired old syntheses show their cracks. The signs are that the liberal consensus that seemed to be so stable is now experiencing renewal and change, thanks to new forms of international dialogue.

The Industrial Revolution left a legacy of undefended intellectual bastions. While we are still trying to update the philosophy of liberal democracy, globalization is upon us. What has happened to commodities is happening to ideas: Barriers against trade burst open, currencies flit from corner to corner of the globe, old consumer habits fade before invasive floods of industrial merchandise. By the same process, we see the dissolution of categories. Closed spheres are opened, once impregnable vantage points are taken by storm. Conversation is becoming general.

For some the normlessness and loss of identity are terrible; others are exhilarated by a keener self-awareness. If they were responsible for public policy, however, they may be less happy. Conflicts appear between different ideas of well-being. This is always the case in a plural democracy, and we have seen that one of the stock solutions to moral conflict is to tolerate ambiguity. But if globalization breaks down isolated pockets of thought, keen blasts of criticism uncover ambiguity. Already social theory has lost any local hegemony it had. The French are here, talking to each other and to us about our own ideas about welfare and justice, as well as about theirs. The Germans have been here for some time, talking about the public sphere. The Italians are here, talking politics. The Spanish are here, talking about conflict and conciliation. That is just the Europeans starting to talk to each other; the Japanese are also here, the voices of the Koreans and the Chinese, to say nothing of Peru, Brazil, and other Eastern and South American nations that will be heard. European voices will not dominate future conversations. Politics will not be able to be excluded. International exposure forces intellectual adjustments; rivals and strangers learn to speak together. New convergences appear, language is cleansed, and new definitions are tried. It all sounds very hopeful.

In a moving analysis, Victor Perez-Diaz draws attention to Europe's effort to make up for its separate languages, separate histories, and unshared, even hostile, memories. He points particularly to our need to reconstruct our relationships with our respective histories.

> In the United States, the Americans share the narrative of the foundation of the old colonies, the saga of the War of Independence and the Constitution, and two hundred years of (fundamentally) institutional continuity based on these origins. In Europe, nations tell stories which, familiar to one, are foreign to the next, stories that are like inverted mirror images. The glory of one led to the decline of another, the revolutionary expansion of one was the invasion of another, the divine Church of one was the scourge of heretics to another; the Enlightenment may be seen as imitation or banality; . . . Over time, the hostility and rancour have diminished somewhat; but it is doubtful whether they will ever disappear entirely because they are closely bound up with the founding or defining myths of identity of almost all the European nations. (Perez-Diaz 1994: 14)

This is a Spaniard whose country endured a savage civil war and yet he believes that the part of our history which can unite Western Europe most effectively, in spite of its horrors, is this century's experience of fascist totalitarian states and an appalling war. But he thinks that its ideological unity is very precarious, based, as he says, on "some variant of the democratic and market ideal" (p. 15). No one would dispute his view that this ideal plays a central role in our sense of identity, self-respect, and moral worth, or that it is the democratic ideal that unites Western Europe to the United States. But is he right to think that it is a fragile link?

We will argue to the contrary that the ideals of Western industrial democracy are far from fragile. The fear that they need protection is part of their strength. We will show how well they are entrenched and the contradiction and yawning gaps that have to be tolerated without demur.

TOTAL OBJECTIVITY

The official discourse on poverty needs objectivity because it must make standard measures. But now a call for political honesty is made in the name of total objectivity: The discourse on poverty has to be deideologized. Some comments on Bourdieu's *La Misère du monde* illustrate the demand for an impossible posture.

Bourdieu claims that his edited work is primarily ethnographic and not argumentative. However, a formally favorable review (Genestier 1994) completely undermines the claims. The editor says that he is letting the poor people he is writing about speak for themselves, but the reviewer complains that he frames them in a highly constrained interview context. He wishes to dissociate himself from the accepted categorization of poverty, but he chooses his subjects according to their lack of material things; by taking welfare recipients for his survey he complicitly accepts the official definitions that he wants to be seen as rejecting; bewailing cultural impoverishment, he confirms the superior value of the learned culture.

Yes, to be sure, says Philippe Genestier, trying to give a "nonviolent" and attentive hearing, the interviewing team are open to what they are being told; they scrupulously base their analyses on the data; their method is designed to protect them from the well-known distortions of surveys. Nonetheless, they import their own notions into their explanatory system, they superimpose their own clear-cut schemas on the confused notions of the interview subjects, they boringly replace the rich background of daily life with the familiar diagnosis of symbolic and institutional violence. How can they justify their selection of what is really important in all of this? The researchers have imposed their grid on the data. Their own mental habits and categories have predetermined the results. The inquiry has set its sights so that it can only read the answers according to the criteria of the dominant culture. The method of inquiry has locked the subjects of the interviews into a predetermined posture: They are posed in classic attitudes of lament and indictment. Between separate worlds, how can there be judgment?

With a two-pronged strategy the reviewer deflates the researchers' pretensions. One prong looks for signs that the high standards claimed to govern the research have been abandoned. The other prong declares that the original method was not capable of annulling the researchers' presuppositions anyway and that these have rendered the research valueless.

The first prong seems fair enough: The researcher ought to have stood by his method. The second prong seems to be quite unfair: It exalts an impossible "view from nowhere" (Nagel 1986). The researcher is not allowed to take up any position. He is not even allowed to have a prior conception of what it is all about.

Globalization undermines empires of all kinds and brings any two discourses into confrontation on equal terms by exposing the underlying premises. It makes a hard world for research. No one set of assumptions will pass the test. Disgust with domination and pressure for equality and fairness can make any judgment unacceptable if it is successful enough to monopolize the arena and exclude other possibly valid judgments. When the same distrust of domination is applied to reasoning, argument dies. Globalization can bring all formulations of public policy to this bar, all premises are to be tried on the same charge, the accusation of having an opinion or a theory. In the face of totalizing relativism, what can you say? How can you avoid constructing the policy issues, either from a consistent, underlying bias or from a ragtag set of received ideas? Either way, the critic wins. When the critic finds that the declared premises do not match what is said, or that the argument has shifted to a new, hidden set of premises, the writer is in trouble not for sloppy writing but for cheating. For some critics any kind of schematizing or organizing of data is wrongful, to be resisted as an attempt to impose domination. It is fair to ask the relativizing reviewer what sort of writing would be acceptable.

In truth, there was a new approach to poverty in Bourdieu's book. It was an idea typical of an anthropologist, and, open and nonviolent though he was, the reviewer innocently imposed his own preconceived idea. What Genestier missed, in interview after interview, was the respondents showing a common trouble: They suffered not from material lack, not from want of things, but from problems about other people, the absence of certain desired presences, and the too-intrusive official presence of others. The form that poverty took in this book had a lot to do with the poor person's lack of control over other people.

THE OLD DIALOGUE ABOUT THE PERSON

The Anglo-Saxon philosophers may have succeeded for a time in establishing an imperium based on their own classification of social problems, as Kenneth Boulding once said they expected to do (Boulding 1970). Durkheim and his colleagues, opposed to the concept of economic man, constructed their own abstract view of society. They started to expand Kant's universal categories of perception to include a social category, necessary for a preeminently social being. But while they found themselves addressing mainly their own colleagues of *L'Année Sociologique*, the rest of the world went on discussing perception without reference to society and society without reference to the self. In the practical terms of successfully rooting a theory in teaching practice, Durkheim lost against Kant in the schools of philosophy. And the English proved his point about thought being embedded in practice when they allowed *Homo œconomicus* to continue to reign over their institutions.

But now the old struggle about the nature of the person is renewed. French social scientists deplore the transitory and unessential character of other persons in the social sciences (Caillé 1986, 1989, 1993). The process of justification is the basis of the social bond; without justification, knowledge can have no grounding; justification involves dialogue and presupposes the presence of others before whom to be justified. A social theory that ignores the presence of others in its account of reason must fail, because it cannot say how agreement is reached (Boltanski and Thévenot 1991: 48).

Brought back thus to Durkheim's neglected program, in chapter 2 we will propose a social theory about the acceptability of social theories. We will examine the implicit psychological theory that seems to be accepted in neoclassical economics, but we will not join the economists who love to berate each other for neglect of modern psychology, and we will not take sides in arguments between economists.

CHAPTER TWO

The Strong Presence
of *Homo Œconomicus*

HOMO ŒCONOMICUS

Ancient historians and anthropologists often report a remote civilization where human behavior is explained by a microcosm of the universe. For the people of that civilization, intellectual inquiry is free only to the extent that it conforms to the system of thought; the laws of the mind and the laws of society stand in fixed harmony with the laws of the stars and the planets. When such a microcosm is not only an intellectual scheme but is also adopted for the practical working of society, it becomes all-pervasive. It explains the way the world is, and does it so completely and satisfactorily that it is not possible to step outside it and think differently, or even to see its influence. The person whose life and thought take place inside the microcosm feels quite free and does not notice the constraint.

The idea of rational economic man works like a microcosm in our professional social thought. It comes out of economics, but we will show in this and following chapters that its hold on Western social thought has to do with many other institutional settings and is much more comprehensive. It acts like a psychological theory, but this is not how it works in economics.

Homo œconomicus is a male person, sometimes a homunculus inside each of us, sometimes a giant incorporating the whole of society or the world. Our pervasive microcosm to whose outlines all our explanations are required to fit is a quintessential stranger; he has no family or friends, no personal history; his emotions are not like ours; we don't understand his language, still less his purposes. The popular model of economic man is a rank outsider, but we model our questions about ourselves on the idea we have of him.

How was *Homo œconomicus* foisted on us? In spite of his elegant foreign name, he is selfish and unmannered, brutish as Caliban, naïve as Man Friday. We all love to speak scathingly of him. Judging from the bad press he receives, we actually dislike him a lot and cannot believe anyone could really be so greedy and selfish. He is logical, but even that is unattractive. His shadow stretches across our thoughts so effectively that we even use his language for criticizing him.

Economists need not fear that what follows is an attack on their profession. Economic man is an easy target for attack, with retaliatory complaints that he is drawn wrong. Our subject is about his origins: Where did someone without social attributes come from in the first place, and why has he expanded from a small, theoretical niche to become an all-embracing mythological figure? He is like a republican parallel to the imperial microcosm of former civilizations.

THE JEALOUS MICROCOSM

The idea of microcosm is that of a powerful analogy that replicates itself in a series of concentric circles. It is best described by theological or oriental examples. A. M. Hocart, in his 1936 classic, *Kings and Councillors*, after talking about Indian ritual, added,

> [T]he analogy of macrocosm and microcosm is found at an earlier stage in Babylonia. The analogy of man and the universe was known in the Stoics and to the Chinese. The doctrine that "man is a universe in little and the universe a man in great" was a favourite with Jewish thinkers, especially the Cabala . . . The fact is we cannot get away from the idea of worlds in little. (Hocart 1970: 67–68)

The energy a reigning idea exerts to stop alternative ideas from flourishing in its presence is like a monarch who is suspicious of supplanters, a banyan tree that kills off the saplings in its shade. The king's body was the model of the universe in medieval Europe: As the king is to the kingdom, so the parts of the body recapitulate political relationships, as right hand to left hand, head to hands, and so on. However, such a hierarchical stock of metaphors would be quite at odds with the egalitarian universe modeled by economic man. With us it has been overthrown and thoroughly supplanted.

A well-entrenched Western exceptionalism allows us to nullify the idea that Hocart was talking about a universal mode of thought. Those people, far away and long ago, thought in that mold. Because he drew all his examples from ritual and mythology, they sound bizarre to our ways of thinking. These ideas were in thrall to religion, but ours are secular and free. They were answerable to a controlling hierarchy; we are egalitarian and answerable to ourselves. Consequently, it would be thought, microcosmic thinking is of antiquarian interest but has no relevance to ourselves.

THE JEALOUS MEME

This is how Hocart failed to receive the recognition his original and learned insights deserved. That he failed is the view expressed by Rodney Needham in his introduction to the English translation of *Kings and Councillors* (Hocart 1970). Hocart wanted to draw attention to a universal human mode of thought that related society, the body, and the physical universe in the same scheme. But his discovery was thought to be about archaic or exotic forms of behavior, cases of primitivism under which we used to once labor in medieval Christian Europe but which now are happily superseded. In fact, an opposing microcosm was already in place. Hocart himself never realized that he was defeated by the very process he was studying.

A microcosm is benign to its loyal followers and mean to rivals. To explain how it works and keeps itself above criticism we can refer to Richard Dawkins's idea of the meme, a replicable, complex idea. The fundamental principle is "that all life evolves by the differential survival of replicating entities . . . the gene, the DNA molecule, happens to be the replicating entity which prevails on our own planet. There may be others. If there are, provided certain conditions are met, they will almost inevitably tend to become the basis for an evolutionary process." He goes on to speculate that "a new kind of replicator has recently emerged on this very planet. It is staring us in the face. It is still in its infancy, still drifting clumsily about in its primeval soup, but already it is achieving evolutionary change at a rate which leaves the old gene panting far behind" (Dawkins 1976: 206). The new kind of replicator he has in mind is the meme. We are now paraphrasing Daniel Dennett: Memes are the cultural units which are the smallest elements that replicate themselves with reliability and fecundity (1991: 201). Although Dennett makes the meme sound like science fiction, he is completely serious. He admits that he is not himself initially attracted by the idea, but he strongly recommends it as a theory of mind.

The two essential characteristics of the meme are, first, that it has the power of replicating itself and, second, that it does so prolifically. Then the microcosmic theories that Hocart described would be excellent examples: The theory that makes the world a microcosm starts with the movement of the planets, or with the body of the king, and rapidly multiplies its exemplars so that the whole universe is replete with the same model, one inside the other or linked by their similarity. There is no room left for any rival theory. The microcosmic meme is just as greedy and just as active as the gene.

Dennett finds that what is really interesting about the replicatory power of certain complex sets of ideas are the exceptions. Something happens, and the evolutionary process comes to a standstill, or decays, or splits into two or more streams. We will be showing examples of this too, and offering explanations both of how the energy to replicate is fueled and how it can be lost. We also can benefit from the careful avoidance of teleology in genetic theory. The replications are not in themselves good for anything. An opening appears, and the meme moves in, applying its replication of itself to the whole scenario. Dawkins and Dennett would say that it does so for its own sake, not in order to achieve anything other than its own survival and continued power of self-replication. That seems to rule out functionalist teleology, but it tends to introduce another teleology, the intentions and ambitions of the gene to further its own reproduction. The meme case is different from the gene case, not least because it is people who carry the fertile, parasitic ideas. It is they, not the meme, who take the path of least resistance; they, not the meme, who think up replications and who appeal to each other to accept their plausibility. People do the spreading and infecting and dominating, on their own behalf, to further their own intentions.

We do not have to adopt Dawkins's funny language that attributes selfishness to genes. It may be a useful trick in genetics, but for talking about the replications of ideas we must insist that the meme has no intentions of its own. It is only by a jokey analogy that we shall be calling it greedy and seeming to attribute to it the emotion of jealousy. It is a pity, but perhaps in examining a present-day powerful microcosm as an example of a meme we might be wise to avoid the latter term, but it may turn out to be irresistible. A seductive path has opened up, with hopeful, bandwagoning opportunities offering increasing returns to explicatory effort; in short, a new meme about thought styles.

We should perhaps attest to our own thoughtfulness and seriousness by drawing distinctions among kinds of memes. We are interested in political memes that dominate the mode of thought about governance and the good society. Of those, we are interested in memes that have proved their success by infiltrating most of the area of political thought and particularly those which have so well subdued resistant strains that theories of the body and the earth and theories of the soul and of social and political life are all replicated in the same way. In short, we are interested in the invasive and controlling influence of a successful microcosm, in the secret of its success, and in why the microcosm is occasionally supplanted.

The more ancient or exotic the analogies of microcosms that Hocart cited, the more outlandish they seemed and the less could they have been tolerated as an account of a universal mode of thought, which he wanted to suggest. The lack of credibility in his idea could serve as an example of the meme's refusal to allow a rival to succeed. A theory about universal microcosmic thinking habits could never have received more than glancing attention from marginal corners of the intellectual world that was being molded through the nineteenth and twentieth centuries. Now things are different—the view is less obstructed and there is a chance of something different getting through.

In vain did Hocart try to recruit science to his thesis, referring to the germ theory of disease in terms of microcosmic parallels thus: "[J]ust as a germ cell bears upon it the impress of its parents, . . . so would terrestrial life bear upon it the impress of mother universe. And further, just as from an examination of a germ cell we would be able to form an idea of the leading characters of the parent, . . . so would we from an examination of terrestrial life be able to gain a knowledge of its parent the universe" (Hocart 1970: 68, quoting Francis Younghusband in the *Hibbert Journal*). Scientists were actually quite happy to let each other make analogic leaps in their own work. In his account of Darwinian theory Stephen Jay Gould (1981) cites derisively the widely accepted notion that the changing shape of the human fetus in the womb recapitulates the main stages of animal evolution. Bruno Latour is prepared to talk about Pasteur as introducing a microbial microcosm of society in his theory of disease transmission and even to suggest that the form of society changed in response to the idea (Latour 1988). Such examples rely on metaphors for the links in their arguments, but metaphors can be roots for anything whatsoever. To be convinced, we would still need to know the mechanism by which the acceptable cosmic metaphor takes root and why a myriad of other metaphors fall by the wayside.

In what does unacceptability consist? An idea is unacceptable if it patently does not fit experience, or else because it is threatening. Other people's microcosms, when presented as descriptions of foreign delusions, are not threatening. It is different to imply that we, here and now, are thinking in terms controlled by a dominant and very jealous microcosm. Hocart's examples offered no threat. They were not only totally bizarre, they were in the realm of ritual and mythology.

In the 1930s it made sense to suggest that the idea comes first and that social understanding is rooted in it. Nowadays the weight of opinion in the history of ideas goes the other way: The social practice roots the idea, and the idea withers if it is deprived of that sustaining soil. To exploit Hocart's initial insight we shall have to examine case after case of practice, entrenched in useful institutions, each practice using a shared idea as a latch to tie up with another practice, entrenched in another set of practices, and so on, the practices combining to protect from threat a web of intellectual justifications.

A TOOL-TO-THEORY HEURISTIC

To make our argument strong, we would be wise to do some further latching on our own account. The following view of the reigning ideas concerning well-being derives from current theories of scientific innovation that emphasize the growth of ideas embedded in laboratory practice and scientific institutions (Kuhn 1977). In the same way, social theories are embedded in economic practices and institutions. The question of why a particular paradigm should prove stronger than the rest turns into a question about the strength of the institutions in which it is grounded. The growth of the idea of economic man conforms to theories about scientific discovery in which tools have an active role and can directly inspire new theories.

By tools, Gerd Gigerenzer means the tools of justification, analytical or physical. He illustrates microcosm with the mechanical clock that, when it became the indispensable tool for astronomical research, made the universe itself understandable as a mechanism which the divine clock maker set going (Gigerenzer 1992: 332). One after another he gives examples, starting with techniques of statistical inference and hypothesis testing, leading to what is known as the "inference revolution" and on to theories of memory, judgment, information processing, rationality, and more. He presents each with its distinctive homunculus statistician in charge of the mental activity in question. In each case a parallel is drawn between the process of testing theory and the character of the human mind, the microcosm growing out of the tools in use.

It is a pity that he likes to call it the tool-to-theory heuristic, for that is not a new idea, and he himself cites a distinguished list of predecessors:

> Only recently scholars have moved from looking at science
> through the lens of theory and data towards an integrated

view which considers daily laboratory practice (e.g. Danziger 1990; Galison 1987; Gooding, Pinch, and Schaffer 1989; Hacking 1983). . . . The classical view of tools in scientific discovery is that they generate new data, which in turn can lead to new theories. But our thesis depicts tools as having an even more active role in discovery. We argue that new tools can directly, rather than through new data, inspire new theories. (Gigerenzer and Goldstein 1996: 131)

In this essay Gigerenzer and Goldstein have uncovered the processes of autopoiësis, or self-reproduction. As far as we know, their approach is distinguished in the philosophy of science for, after first buckling the process of ideas into the social process—which is a common achievement—going on to show feedback between the one and the other. At its simplest, the people organize for doing something, they become habituated to the tools they make for judging their work, the regular usage makes them ready to accept an idea based on the proven practice, new theories can take off from this steady foundation, the new theories confirm the value of the practice, and further new theories on the same model will be acceptable. Thinking is possible because it is stabilized by shared practices; social life is possible because it is stabilized by thinking. The snake's tail is in the snake's mouth, and a dynamic circle of interaction is complete. Once the pieces of the microcosm have been put together, a metaphor works because it is compatible with a relevant practice and takes its direction from that compatibility. By extension, an idea acquires replicative power when other institutions can gain support from its success.

According to the assumption that ideas come first, we could suppose that the famous Chinese model of the universe started from a cosmological idea about Heaven. It would then have generated theories about colors, time, astronomy, and the weather, modeling all activity on the place of the emperor as Son of Heaven. Likewise, we assume that our own medieval model of the king's body as microcosm of the kingdom started as a cosmological theory about God that embraced politics and religion and daily practice. But according to the tool-to-theory heuristic, the movement would more likely have been in the other direction. The Chinese microcosm would have started from calendrical reckoning; the medieval microcosm perhaps from warfare. We will show that our economic man emerged from a piece of secular, nonpolitical theorizing rooted in agricultural practice. The law of diminishing marginal utility gained its power to explain from its practical use in necessary calculations.

The comparison of microcosms suggests that they work very well, in spite of what will always seem to outsiders to be a shaky empirical basis with many hypothetico-deductive errors. The Chinese emperor was thought to be so intimately connected with the changing seasons and the movements of the sun and moon that if he deviated from his role, droughts or typhoons or earthquakes would result. As in economics, the best predictions are made after the event. It is easy to sneer at post hoc forecasting. Remember that modern meteorological offices in industrial societies continually come under fire for poor success in trying to predict the future a few days before it becomes the present. And so it is fair to allow that the Chinese microcosm was no less a theory even if it sometimes got the weather wrong.

Most microcosms, including economic man, have a political aspect. Perhaps other grand microcosmic theories were established in a similar way. The idea of microcosm provides a mode of abstraction from the smaller to the greater and back again. At the same time it gives the principles for prescribing good behavior and provides the principles for theorylike predictions about the interactions between humans and the natural world. The origins and evolution of microcosms are difficult to study; we are usually not able to be present through the process. But in this case we have the records, and we know that Economic Man became a microcosm by developing from tool to theory along the path of institutions. Once it became a theory of the mind, its proliferation was assured.

DIMINISHING MARGINAL SATISFACTION

The essence of the idea was a self-quenching mechanism by which a person's desires switch off when satisfied. Ricardo (1772–1823) used a theory of diminishing marginal returns to additional doses of capital and labor applied to land. Such a simple and incontrovertible principle was easy to apply to humans: The more you have had of something you like, the weaker is your desire for another dose of it, an internal seesaw effect susceptible to mathematical expression.

Models of equilibria had been used for a long time in eighteenth-century political economy. Against protectionist policies designed to keep stocks of gold in the country, David Hume (1711–1776) argued that each country's exports automatically come into balance by the effect of gold flows acting on domestic price levels, the first systematic account of the role of prices in achieving equilibrium in international trade (Hume 1752). The Swiss mathematician Daniel Bernouilli (1700–1782) made an early statement of diminishing marginal utility in the context of probability calculations of risk (Bernouilli 1738). He proposed that the utility of wealth increases at a decreasing rate, but the notion was not worked into a flow model of the economy. Putting marginal utility and the principles of equilibrium together took a long time, and the law of satiable wants did not become a central idea until the so-called marginalist revolution of the 1870s.

All at once three thinkers independently produced models of the economy in which the wheels of trade are turned by buyers' demand, with prices as the pivot and supply damped down by lower prices reflecting the principle of diminishing marginal utility: in England W. S. Jevons, in *The Theory of Political Economy* (1871); in Austria Carl Menger, in *Grundsätze der Volkswirtschaftslehre* (1871); and in Switzerland Léon Walras, in *Éléments d'économie politique pure* (1874). The shift was to apply to utility the principle of diminishing marginal returns that Ricardo had applied to land. The buyer has enough when the law of satiability brings him to the price at which it is not satisfying to buy another increment of the thing; enough is enough. With the responsiveness of demand to prices, the model of market equilibrium took shape. Introducing wants and desires was a revolutionary shift in the theoretical scene that had formerly focused on the relationships among factors of production.

It is easy to see why the analogy was intellectually irresistible. From the history of ideas two reasons suggest themselves. First, utility theory was an idea that was easy to ground in physical nature. The human body provides a source of powerful analogies. Any textbook about utility naturalizes the theory, usually by reference to the food analogy—appetite declines with eating—or to the medicine analogy—good medicines taken in excess become poisons. Alfred Marshall, staying close to the Ricardian origins of marginalism, used the agricultural analogy. He said that the law of satiable wants or of "*diminishing marginal utility*, holds a priority of position to the *law of diminishing returns from land*, which has however a priority in time. So one can say: 'the return' of pleasure which a person gets from each additional dose of a commodity diminishes till at last a margin is reached at which it is no longer worth his while to acquire any more of it" (Marshall 1890: 93). By using the words *doses* and *return* he deliberately combined the pleasure case with Ricardo's agricultural case.

Incidentally, this shows how mistaken is the popular idea of economic man's rapacity in the quest for profit. From the beginning of economic theory, the rational economic being was never seen as greedy. According to utility theory, he is subject to some kind of self-regulatory principle that tells him when he has had enough. His wants are not limitless: Diminishing marginal utility is the name of the self-equilibrating principle of psychic restraint. The name describes it but does not explain how it works. Explanation is not necessary, because the idea has been so thoroughly naturalized. We all understand it. There are many situations in which we have direct and uncontroversial experience of its validity. Its power to save on explanation costs is another source of the meme's power to proliferate.

The reference to nature sustains plausible intuitions. There is the case of the field, absorbing so much labor and fertilizer and, after a certain point, giving a diminishing return to each new input. The theory can proceed unchallenged, protected by the tacit assumption that the regulatory controls come from inside the person, as they come from inside the field. In the case of the cultivated field, agronomy and soil chemistry would give a coherent chain of reasoning. In the case of the body, physiology would do the same.

REINFORCED MULTIPLE COSMIC EFFECTS

A microcosm does well if it can serve as a model of the universe, of the empire, of the mind, and of how the models interact at different levels. The secret of its replication is that the more it can do, the more deeply it becomes entrenched. The interesting questions about scientific discovery are not how the discovery was made in the first place but how it became institutionalized. Gigerenzer has argued that a tool of investigation becomes most effectively justified when it can provide a double metaphor of how the world reflects the workings of the mind (Gigerenzer 1991). He remarks that "once the mechanical clock became the indispensable tool for astronomical research, the universe itself came to be understood as a kind of mechanical clock, and God as a divine watchmaker" (p. 255). His main examples of this two-way naturalization are from cognitive science and inferential statistics. These can be seen as modern versions of antique microcosm principles.

Following Gigerenzer's principle, the theory of utility was set from the outset to grow into a microcosm, because it made self-regulating wants of the individual match the self-regulating mechanism for the economy. On the supply side, production has to keep average costs from being excessive in relation to prices, but when wants start to be satisfied demand and prices fall, supply and demand come to an equilibrium price, and market is stabilized. The rational individual buyer is surrounded by a pale penumbra of wants that are at the point of fading out. He is not strictly alone, for he is surrounded by prices, which he watches. Prices represent other people and their wants. The whole purpose and use of the model is technical and theoretical. The rational being in the middle of market theory has little or nothing to do with prescribing politics or morals. First the political economy was developed as a homeostatic model, and then the psyche of the consumer was invoked to link up demand and supply in order to stabilize the system and make the machinery work.

Then the political lessons easily fell into place. The principle of marginal utility was a model well suited to justify a Whig policy of unrestricted trade. The self-equilibrating processes did not allow for resources to go unused or wants unsatisfied. Confidence in the theory of the market led economists to assume that if there was unemployment it would be voluntary. Like the voluntary refusal to buy goods that were regarded as too expensive, work would be refused if the wage was (rightly or wrongly) considered too low. Within this theory there was no way to interpret the experience of massive unemployment.

The model of demand was too simple, too closed, and too static. In rethinking the problems of the 1920s depression and mass unemployment, Keynes improved the model by adding the principle of the marginal propensity to consume. Previously, consumers' expenditures would have been expected to rise proportionately with every rise in income, but Keynes postulated that every rise in the level of income was accompanied by a less-than-proportional rise in expenditure. Ineffective demand caused consumption to lag behind rising income levels. Keynes's invention of the marginal propensity to consume sounds like the same psychic model, only slightly developed. But true to the theoretical tradition, it is not a model of the psyche. The gesture toward psychology is decorative: It gives continuity but does not matter, for the theory is supposed to pass quite another kind of empirical test. The problem was set because the market was not being cleared. Keynes showed that consumption is determined by income as well as by prices and that the first model of consumer behavior failed not because of research in the field of psychology but because it did not connect the different parts of market theory that it had been designed to link.

The phrase "marginal propensity to consume" suggests that some internal mechanism like diminishing marginal utility regulated the consumer's underspending. (Never a hearty feeder, the consumer seemed to have become that bad-mannered guest who does not even finish what is on his plate. For some reason his appetite is more fastidious than had been supposed.) But speculation about money illusion and the difference between real and money wages were a distraction. Marginal propensity to consume is not a theory about the propensities of consumers; it is about the monetary system that has been deprived of the demand of persons who would otherwise have been willing consumers.

HOW ECONOMIC MAN CAME TO STAY

The outsider to economics trying to understand utility theory is particularly struck by the intuitive leaps between levels. In the history of the subject, theoretical development and empirical testing fed each other normally at the market level; the connection between market and the other levels existed only in the imagination. Ultimately the plausibility of the whole theoretical edifice still rests on a popular but untested set of analogic recapitulations.

An economic theory of satiety and diminishing desire is a real theory, with predictions about economic behavior. It can be tested with market data, and it works. Though it sounds as if it is based on physiology, the self-restraint exhibited by the buyer in the market is not part of a physiological or psychological theory. Its prima facie plausibility is a theory not about hunger or thirst but about how markets behave, about quantities, profits, and losses on the market. Hunger and desire are analogies. They carry the meaning from physiological needs to market prices, but they are not articulated in any theory. The theory of market is naturalized. It comes to rest on the physiology of the human person, which seems to ground it in nature. It is naturalized as a threefold microcosm: The bodily organism is used as a model for the psyche, and both psyche and organism are used as a model for the market. All three are rationalized by the idea of hierarchies of needs.

1. The body has needs—for water, food, and sleep; its needs for rest conform to the succession of nights and days and to the movements of the sun and stars. Some bodily needs are more exigent and must be satisfied first, while others can wait; internal principles of organization bring them into order and balance. What these internal principles of physical existence are does not matter; they are secondary elaborations that belong to another department of analysis. If you must inquire, go find a physiologist.

2. Likewise, the consumer's psyche has wants, some more insistent than others; parallel self-regulating principles bring them into equilibrium. What the principles of psychic health are

does not matter to the economist; the theory of psychic needs belongs to another department. If you must inquire, ask the specialist . . . but who would that be?

3. Likewise again for the anthropomorphized market, the consumer's psyche (established by its analogy with the body) enters as part of the mechanism of self-regulation: Diminishing marginal utility has its role in the theory of the market, and when it comes to knowing more about market behavior, the specialists are economists.

As easily as we can detect logical leaps in the theory of the Chinese emperor's influence on climate, we can see logical leaps in the functional connections among the microcosmic levels of utility theory. Each level works on different principles, and any similarity or match there may be between them is an artificial and unjustifiable construct imposed on the materials. There is empirical testing of the theory, but it has nothing to do with giving people standard platefuls of food and measuring when appetite fades, or with seeing whether joy does diminish proportionately to additional increments. The strict empirical tests are concerned with prices, quantities, and profit and loss in the market. The technology of inquiry into consumer behavior belongs to the economists, and the data they examine to improve their theory have to do with market behavior.

THE PHYSIOLOGY
OF *HOMO ŒCONOMICUS*

It has to be admitted that *Homo œconomicus* does not fulfill the function for which he was invented. His spending does not help the market to recover after a fall, as it was expected to. The economists have no idea why he does not spend, but in a depression they wish he would, and in a period of inflation they wish he would not. In default of a theory, they just watch him. When he refrains from buying domestic hardware they feel worried; when he launches out and buys consumer durables, they cheer up at symptoms of economic recovery. A new person is now threshing around unpredictably inside the theory. He has become more interesting and attractive, not so cool and logical, more nervous and excitable. He is more like one of us, but, most notably, he does not serve the purpose he was invented for, which was to explain the market. In default, he has developed a new role. George Katona (1901–1981) invented "psychological economics," inspired by gestalt psychology. He helped found Survey Research Center at the University of Michigan and conducted surveys to measure changes in consumer confidence for short-run predictions. Now the consumer is a signal: He provides the data for the consumer index and tells the economists what to expect.

One of the things that has gone wrong can be laid at the door of the original physiological model that fooled us into thinking the constraints are internal. The constraints on consumer behavior are assumed to come from inside him, like the flows of saliva and digestive juices from inside the body. As we said at the start, *Homo œconomicus* was tricked out like a perfect stranger, with no ties and no commitments. At an early stage the prospect of the consumer running wild and spending his all would only have been envisaged as a pathology. For him to give way intemperately to lust or gluttony would not have been rational behavior—animals do not eat more than they need. Nor was it envisaged that his appetite could fade completely. But in the late 1920s the stranger sitting down at the table looked anorexic. The theory of marginal utility would have been in a mess but for help from an unexpected quarter.

The work of Ernst Engel (1821–1896), a social-reformer statistician, did not become important until after the Great Depression, when the theory of the market and of the consumer's contribution to the economic system most needed strengthening. Engel discovered a relationship between a household's income and allocation of expenditure, now called the Engel Curve. According to Engel's Law, households with higher incomes spent proportionately more on food, but the share of food in the household budget varied inversely with income. The systematic study of the Engel Curve started only in 1935. Now Engel's Law is the best-established empirical reality in economics: It shows how expenditure is hierarchized; it prioritizes the place of food in the budget; and so it supports the dependence of the utility model on physiology. The household budget imposes logic on desires, and the logic is in harmony with the original idea of self-regulatory physiological needs.[1]

Engel supposed that there was a fairly smooth development of wants from satisfying hunger and thirst to satisfying other needs.

---

1. Engel worked with the French sociologist Frédéric Le Play. Extrapolating from persons to whole nations, Engel inferred that with economic development agriculture would decline relative to other sections of the economy. After relative income, other variables were added: family size, composition, and the like. Income elasticity defines luxuries, and so forth. Expenditure items are called luxuries, necessities, and inferior goods, depending on whether the income elasticity is greater than 1, between 0 and 1, or less than 0. The Keynesian consumption function may be considered an extension of the Engel Curve.

Ultimately, on this assumption, the whole demand schedule could theoretically be drawn as a satisfying of interdependent private needs and prerequisites for other needs. But though this works empirically, it gives the wrong clues about utility by affirming that it is a feature of the behavior of an aggregated living person. What is wrong with the continuous line from basic needs to all other wants is that it allows us to be complacent about the naturalized version of the solipsist consumer.

Marshall considered utility a theory for explaining how markets are cleared, not a theory of how human life is sustained. In summarizing Bernouilli's theorem, he said that the principle does not start to apply until the income is enough to support life (Marshall 1890: 6). So, as you would expect for a theory of value, diminishing marginal utility is a theory about wants, not about needs.

This person whom we have called the stranger in our midst seems immune to attack because he is protected by replications of a theory of diminishing wants in economics, mapped onto physiology and onto the psyche. If more demonstrations were necessary, remember that the pattern of his desires was originally mapped onto the productivity of the land. Now the servant is emperor. Microcosm is the principle of group-think. By microcosmic links between one branch of learning and another, economic man has become as natural as any other natural fact.

SAYING FAREWELL

Economists who want to improve or lose the neoclassical paradigm think that it is up to them, that it is their problem and all they have to do is listen to what is going on in the other social sciences. A central theme of this volume denies their responsibility, or at least asks it to be shared. Economic man has been welcomed everywhere. If the economists look into the other social sciences they will just see his face in the window. In recent years Geoffrey Hodgson has eloquently attacked the dominant theory, but we should ask him frankly what difference it would make for economists to take Freudian analysis on board, or other branches of psychology (Hodgson 1988: 60–62). Economists do not really have a psychological theory at all, or a theory of wants, only a theory of the market. For this they have a very powerful analytical tool kit. It should not be necessary to say farewell to the whole box of tools.

Hodgson has shown with perfect clarity how the analysis of rational choice serves a particular political commitment. The real question should be whether the analytical tool can be used to serve several political goals instead of one unique set. Our critical attention should be on kinds of commitments and the means used to protect them. The first step is to examine the currently acceptable idea of the person and to work on it to make it able to play a more complex and flexible theoretical role.

The dominant idea is simple: It could be drawn as concentric circles, with ego in the middle of progressively weakening spheres of influence. Other egos are not in the picture, or if they are to be seen, they are minor, faint images. Anything that diminishes the theoretical autonomy of ego is seen as a threat. Though economic man fits well with professional needs for thinking about us, he is still the wrong model for the rational being. He arrived as a stowaway in our theoretical baggage. As insidiously as a computer virus, he makes our inquiries about our well-being conform to the fiction about himself. He is not located in economics; pervasively, in one field after another, the ideas we have about poverty and well-being—and about justice, educational theory, charity, and risk—reinforce each other, and in each sphere his familiar face contributes to the aura of intellectual respectability.

CHAPTER THREE

Communication Needs
of Social Beings

TRYING TO IMAGINE A SOCIAL BEING

A social being has one prime need—to communicate. Because it is a social being, everything in its genetic inheritance, especially its intelligence, must be equipped to read the signals and to signal back to the others of its kind. There is nothing in the description of *Homo œconomicus* that indicates these basic capacities and needs. Not surprisingly, the empty cipher that does service as a person needs to be supplemented occasionally to make room for the social functions. It is usually done additively.

One favorite supplement is to divide the person into two, one-half private and one-half social. Durkheim used the phrase *Homo duplex* for the idea that a person is always split between egoist principles, which correspond to the economists' idea of economic man, and moral conscience, which refers a person's decisions to the larger social unit (Durkheim 1995: 15–16, 265–67, 134–36). Opinion researchers, whose profession is to tell us about ourselves, make a similar division between needs: Some, the so-called lower needs, are met by physical satisfactions; others, the higher needs, are less immediate. Implicitly this divides the person between material and immaterial parts, a duplex creature, half spiritual–half physical, or half human–half animal.

The spiritual needs are associated with symbolic values; the others are useful necessities. The principle of classification does not work well, because it is impossible to make a clear distinction between instrumental and symbolic. Even useful things have symbolic value. In fact, every single thing symbolizes, especially food, disinfectant sprays, furniture polish, bleaches, houses, clothes, soap, textiles, dyes, metals. The mistake is to focus on the thing emanating its symbols instead of on the life-project for which the person wants that thing. We shall offer first some examples of this style of thought as it shows in opinion surveys and then an alternative based on the idea that tastes, so far from being private, are involved in the communication process.

BREAD IN THE BELLY

Market research is much influenced by Abraham Maslow's idea that the individual person is composed of a spiritual element in an animal body. The two parts can be distinguished, and they generate different kinds of motivations. The animal needs are primary and must be satisfied before ethical, artistic, and spiritual needs can receive attention. This composite being is only able to attend to higher needs when its belly is full. This bread-in-the-belly theory of art and altruism organizes values into an evolving hierarchy. Remembering chapter 2, we note that the theory is supported by a microcosm from natural history: The shift from lower to higher needs recapitulates the evolution of the species from lower to higher species.

In Victorian times, implanting a desire for higher satisfactions was the antidote to the fecklessness of the laboring masses. Malthus himself considered that divinely implanted "mind-growth" would compensate for population growth and the attendant misery. Nowadays the hierarchy of values is used to explain the same thing. Physical needs use up physical resources. The animal in us demands that physical needs be satisfied first, and the poor are by definition short on physical satisfactions. Our contemporary equivalent of "mind-growth" explains why the well-to-do are—allegedly—more deeply engaged with higher and otherworldly issues than are the working classes; they are comfortable enough to attend to their higher needs. It is they who are concerned for the threatened environment and show anxiety about tropical rain forests, the fate of the whales, and the doom of rare small fish. If these count as higher forms of satisfactions, there is more information about the altruists that gives a different explanation, but we will not be ready until chapter 8 to take account of their higher level of education and their marginalization in the power stakes.

For anthropologists, as we said in our first chapter, it is not plausible that the poor are too pressed by hunger and other wants to worry about these higher needs. Many of the peoples they study are poor by any standard but still reflective and interested in art and metaphysical speculation. The theory does not explain why some very rich in industrial countries are interested in neither environmental causes nor metaphysics. Some nonmarket civilizations are built on a culture of tight-belted stoicism; some, on competitive profligacy. Not nature but culture defines what a full belly is, how full it should be, and what is needed to fill it.

Ronald Inglehart has developed Maslow's bread-in-the-belly idea by projecting it onto standard of living. He has divided the public into materialist and postmaterialist (Inglehart 1990), the former focused on problems close at hand and the latter, with a longer span of interest, concerned with more remote issues. On this basis, increasingly liberal attitudes are associated with rising living standards. This would be a comforting thought. If we can only spread the taste for our commodities and the means for buying them around the world, we can hope that racial tensions and oppression of minorities will be reduced. If we ask why it is plausible that standard of living should have this benign effect, the answer refers to a time structure: Primary needs have to be satisfied first. Only after having seen to their own material needs can people afford to look around and help others who are in need. Giving another twist to the argument, Inglehart finds that the higher the general level of comfort the more postmaterialism, including idealism and altruism, flourishes. We said enough in chapter 1 to explain why this is unconvincing.

BASIC CULTURAL NEEDS

Inevitably, the first indicators of standard of living were based on physical needs. The Level of Living Index (Drewnowski and Scott 1966, cited in Erikson 1987) used a typical table of components and indicators of welfare (Table 2). Components were presented in three groups: basic physical needs, basic cultural needs, and higher needs. In the first group were indicators of nutrition,

TABLE 2. SELF-ACTUALIZATION

The Components and Indicators of Welfare in Macro-Oriented Level of Living Research

Groups of Components	Components	Indicators
Basic Physical Needs	Nutrition	• Caloric intake per day, per capita, as a percentage of needs • Total protein intake—grams per day per capita • Percentage of total calories derived from cereals, roots, tubers, and sugars
	Shelter (occupancy of dwellings)	• Magnitude of services from dwellings providing shelter, assessed through quality of dwellings in which the population is housed • Density of occupancy—persons per room in conventional dwellings • Independent use of dwellings—ratio of the number of housing units (in conventional dwellings) to the number of households
	Health (medical care and health services received)	• Access to medical care—percentage of population with access to adequate medical care • Percentage of deaths due to infectious diseases • Proportional mortality ratio—ratio of deaths of those aged 50 and over to total number of deaths
Basic Cultural Needs	Education (education received)	• School–education ratio—percentage fulfillment of enrollment norms • School output ratio—number of graduates to number enrolled • Pupil–teacher ratio—percentage fulfillment of norms
	Leisure and recreation (leisure and recreation enjoyed)	• Leisure time—number of hours free from work per year per capita • Daily newspaper circulation per 1,000 population • Radio and television sets in operation per 1,000 population
	Security (maintenance of security of the person, of the way of life, of the provision for the future)	• Maintenance of the security of the person—incidence of violent deaths per 1,000,000 population per year • Maintenance of the security of the way of life—proportion of the population covered by unemployment and sickness benefits • Maintenance of the security of the provision of the future—proportion of the population covered by old-age pensions or private savings
Higher Needs	Surplus income	• Surplus income above the cost of providing for basic needs, at the actual level of satisfaction

SOURCE: Drewnowski and Scott (1966), cited in Erikson 1987. *The Scandinavian Model: Welfare Studies and Welfare Research*. M. E. Sharpe, Armonk, N.Y., pp. 180–181.

shelter, and health; in the second, education, leisure, and security. A serious flaw in the scheme is that higher needs are assumed to be only met with surplus income, a dubious concept in itself.

Other researchers have sought to counter the limitations of the materialist bias. Allardt (1975) developed an alternative approach to the Swedish model by grouping welfare needs into three kinds: having, meaning control of material and impersonal resources; loving, meaning love, companionship, and solidarity; and being, or self-actualization. His focus is on the necessary conditions for human development. As in the cases of both lower and higher needs, the wants emerge after the basic needs have been satisfied.

In both Erikson's and Allardt's systems the whole concept of wants and needs is encompassed by the individual subject. Allardt has thought that the person may need other people for love and sympathy, but these are requirements for happiness because of what they can do for the personal development of a human being. Allardt is trying to assess degrees of self-actualization without a concept of self. He is trying to have a theory of personal development without any coherent theory of what a person is, so he can only fall back on normative—that is, local—judgment of what a person needs.

In this research on human development and personal capacity the criteria are subjective. The problem is common to most of the current survey work on public attitudes. It follows the traditional bias of psychology, which assumes that wants emanate from individuals and that, basically, individuals are the same the world over. For the sake of objectivity the human person is taken as the aggregated, rational individual, yet what counts as a need is determined by the local climate of (far-from-objective) opinion.

For example, the Institute of Applied Research in Oslo has developed a concept of the "inner quality of life," with four groupings of components: the rating for a high quality of life goes up the more a person is active, such that the more a person has self-esteem, the more he or she has a mutual and close relationship, a sense of togetherness, and a basic mood of joy (Naess 1979, summarized in Erikson 1987). It may be perverse to suggest that not everyone wants a mood of joy all the time. Are we to pity those who have a tragic sense of life? A member of a contemplative religious order can question the universal need for constant activity. "A sense of togetherness" may be a poor translation, but to most people it matters whom they are together with.

We would expect tests for a high quality of life to show criteria of success in relating to those others. This would imply some social framework and not an aggregated individual flourishing in an aggregated society. Without a comparative social dimension, contemporary judgments of quality of life cannot be theoreticized except in the terms of liberal humanist philosophy. This is what is done in most of the essays collected in *The Quality of Life*, edited by Martha Nussbaum and Amartya Sen (1993). The problem is that this philosophy does not represent the good life as it is seen in many parts of the world. It rests respectfully on the entirely local idea of the representative, asocial, unculturated human individual. This would be perfectly acceptable if everybody in the world had *Homo œconomicus* as their cultural ideal. But it leaves out of the count those cultures that are based on ancient hierarchies, and it leaves out the egalitarians who abhor the pursuit of wealth. As to justice, it has no subtlety in dealing with variations on the idea of fairness.

TASTES ARE A COMMUNICATION MECHANISM

According to anthropologists' assumptions, wants and needs do not come from inside the individual person; even their ordering is not a matter of private choice (Douglas 1986a). Other people impose ordering on individual wants by making demands on ego's time and resources. Other people define the short term and the long term. Conventional principles of reciprocity limit how far other people can go, for instance, in delaying repayment of social debts. Social life is a continuous negotiation of acceptable demands, and physical objects only mediate the negotiations.

Assume a calculator that shows what transactions have to be reciprocated and when; assume that demand for objects is part of a chart of social commitments, graded and time-tabled for the year, or the decade, or the lifetime. Chanukah, Christmas, Ramadan, birthdays, anniversaries, and weddings are duly registered, as are initiations, name-days, funerals, visiting the sick with flowers and fruit, retirements, to say nothing of regular hospitality to family and friends. A person wants goods for fulfilling these commitments. Commodities do not satisfy desire; they are only the tools or instruments for satisfying it. Goods are not ends. Goods are for distributing, sharing, consuming, or destroying publicly in one way or another. To focus exclusively on how persons relate to objects can never illuminate the nature of desire. Instead, we should focus on the patterns of alliance and authority that hold between persons, and in all human societies these are marked by the circulation of goods.

Admittedly, it reverses the traditional priorities in economics to suggest that consumption is for other people, not for oneself.

Shifting the explanation of why people want goods transforms the idea of desire in conventional utility analysis but does not invalidate it. The material objects play only an ancillary role. Goods are battle standards: They draw the line between good and evil, and there are no neutral objects. The main objective of consumption is to achieve the desired pattern of social relationships.

If taste formation depended on childhood learning, tastes would be rigid. They actually depend on current interaction with other people. Individuals adopt their tastes in accordance with how they relate to the larger, ongoing system in which they live. As they contemplate their wants and needs, they negotiate with others about how to set priorities and standards of quality—and quantity, too. This does not argue for the social determination of wants. The forms of society are also being negotiated by the same people whose tastes we are studying. Society and tastes are coproduced. As they work together to make their kind of society, the people collaborate over the list of wants and needs they are going to consider acceptable, and they collusively set their judgments of value. Tastes are heavily implicated in the communication process.

Why do we get a laugh out of George du Maurier's satirical attacks on the Aesthetes? Figure 1 shows an intense young bride, admiring a teapot in her hand. At her side stands the much more relaxed bridegroom. The date is 1880. "Oh, Algernon," she says, "Let us live up to it!"

It is not easy to say why the scene is humorous. Is it funny to be inspired to high moral goals by a teapot? Or is it funny that Victorians wanted to be acceptable to their community, or leaders of fashion? Is there a lack of integrity, as if they ought to be

[By Geo. du Maurier.]

Figure 1. "The Six-Mark Teapot." The aesthetic bridegroom asks,
"It is quite consummate, is it not?" The intense bride responds,
"It is, indeed! Oh, Algernon, let us live up to it!" *Source:* du Maurier
1880: 194.

loving the teapot for its own sake? What would be the wrong kind of teapot? And why would it be wrong? At least we can answer that one: In the 1880s the dreaded charge would have been vulgarity. "What! Is the Immaculate impure?—and shall the Academy have coquetted with the unclean!" (Whistler 1967: 131). This wedding-present teapot was evidently the ultimate in refinement.

It may be humorous because nowadays no one worries about vulgarity. The equivalent concern is to avoid being on the wrong side of moral and political standards. Du Maurier presented the six-mark teapot as a riposte to the cult of good taste. The lineup on taste included morals, social institutions, traditions, suitability as marriage partners, membership in clubs, access to credit. The charge of bad taste was used to keep the system closed, to support old money's hegemony against the challenge of the vulgar new rich and against "fortune hunters." But nowadays very little status or wealth is transmitted by marriage. The function of "Keep Out" signs is political alignment.

Figure 2 shows another bridal pair a hundred years later, unpacking their presents. The bride and groom are happy because someone has given them a modem that runs on solar energy. Virtuously, they will not be using fossil fuels when they connect to high-tech networks for electronic mail. The solar modem is not very efficient for their urban lifestyle in the temperate zones, because it works best in arid climates, but it is worth the expense and inconvenience. Already they abstain from using bleaches; soon they will have a pedal-driven hair dryer; they have spotted an advertisement for a lawn mower powered by ocean thermal energy. Now that globalization has drawn the lines internationally, good taste is not at issue. Goods must run the gauntlet not of

Figure 2. The solar modem. (Drawing by Pat Novy)

taste but of moral judgment: They signal that the consumer is for or against women and children, for or against racial minorities, for or against the environment, with the extra subtlety that in place of the shame of poverty, they have to avoid the shame of wealth amid poverty. Events have moved on to show that there is no way of separating instrumental from symbolic objects. By even their most mundane choices the young couple must try to blur their complicity in the Western industrial system.

If the theory of wants and the theory of society are ever to meet, the inherent sociality of the person has to be restored. Without that, economists can have no theory about why people want to buy goods, or why they buy what they buy, or wherein value resides. It is the consumer whose choices turn the wheels of the market, so why should the consumer be a carefully preserved mystery?

ENTITLEMENTS AND INFRASTRUCTURES

What is to be done? There is no current theory of individual needs on which market research and opinion polling can peg out intelligible patterns of behavior. There is no theory of the person to which a theory of individual needs can be pegged. It is a fact that persons, not institutions, enjoy. But quality of life depends on other persons and on what they have done in the past to make it possible for an individual to develop capabilities. A. K. Sen has prioritized two ideas about happiness and commodities: that the individual needs commodities to develop capabilities (Sen 1985) and that poverty is a problem of inadequate infrastructures. In his book on poverty and famine Sen (1981) begins starkly:

> Starvation is the characteristic of some people not having enough to eat. It is not the characteristic of there being not

enough to eat. While the latter can be a cause for the former, it is but one of the many possible causes. Whether and how starvation relates to food supply is a matter for factual investigation. . . .

Food supply statements say things about a commodity (or a group of commodities) considered on its own. Starvation statements are about the relationship of persons to the commodity (or that commodity group). . . . In order to understand starvation, it is, therefore, necessary to go into the structure of ownership. (Sen 1981: 1)

And Sen does, taking us through the history of the great Bengal famine (1942–1943), the Ethiopian famines (1972–1974), drought and famine in the Sahel (1968–1973), and famine in Bangladesh (1974). The entitlements approach concentrates on the ability of people to command food through the legal means available in the society. Told coolly, with consummate literary skill, the story is a tragic account of wrong diagnosis, miscalculation, and mismanagement. In each case the verdict on the cause of the calamity was "food availability decline" (FAD). But FAD was never the cause of the famine: Time and again the food was there, time and again it could have been made available to the people who were without, and time and again human judgment failed, often with good intention but always with catastrophic consequences.

Sen shows that poverty is a problem in the social system that is misdiagnosed as a problem in nature: Floods are blamed, or a late monsoon, or two years of drought, or two successive poor harvests. He shows that once the threat is recognized, the entitlements of some individuals are attacked by erecting a sequence of barriers. The stories are about barriers in towns against the rural poor coming in, rumors and hoarding in the expectation of a rise in prices, price controls that are intended to stop profiteering but actually take food out of the market, legal barriers to movements of food across regions, more hoarding, regulations to stop normal trade, laws against rioting, laws to contain the hungry lest they arrive in town and eat up all that is left. The effects are on individuals who die of starvation, but the analysis is of social systems.

This is a new analysis for public policy. What Sen has called the entitlements approach is focused on the economic, legislative, and political system that controls distribution. It was conceived as a comparative project. By individual entitlements Sen means the rights accorded to a person by the rest of society. He identifies two recurring symptoms of doom: One is attributing the disaster to natural causes, such as FAD, which diverts official attention from the possibility of rescue, and the other is the public battening down of hatches and the locking of gates against the afflicted, which actually causes the worst effects once the famine has started.

After the famine, nothing has been learned. The survivors do not rise up in anger and destroy the system; natural cause is accepted as sufficient explanation; and the same authorities are more strongly established than ever. Most disastrously of all, the system of thought is entrenched, so that next time the telling signs appear, the rulers look carefully at the meteoric conditions and check to be certain that food is available. Finding that it is, they let the rest of the sequence roll on. What the social anthropologist tries to do for a small social unit is here elevated into a method for studying nations. Sen says: "A food-centred view tells us little about starvation" (Sen 1981: 154). By the same token, a health-centered view tells us little about infection and the course of an epidemic. An ego-centered view does not tell us whether the people have the support they need from the way that other people are organized. It says nothing about entitlements.

Entitlements are the ability to be fulfilled as a living being, which means doing what one is capable of doing according to one's individual endowment. The way that the surrounding environment impinges on the individual affects entitlements. This approach directs attention to the supporting infrastructures on which individuals depend. In effect this is what the United Nations Human Development Index (HDI) achieves, to a large degree under Sen's influence.

THE PERSON
IN INTERNATIONAL COMPARISONS

The aim of our work here is not merely to point to the inadequacies of the individualist microcosm—that would be too simple. Eventually, we would like to present the person as a transactor engaged in complex, external exchanges with the environment and with other persons. (We will introduce this idea formally in chapter 4.) The subject of this abstract idea, as we will see, is not the person but the exchange between persons. For describing the person it would be enough to estimate the inputs which he or she can use, the outputs which he or she contributes to the others, and feedback from the exchange activity. The individual, set in a context of other interacting individuals, carries a legacy of institutions from past generations of other persons. Surprisingly, this is the direction in which international comparisons of well-being are moving. Our interest is directed to the quality of the transactions in which the individual can take part, which means taking an interest in a background of inherited possibilities. This is a shift from the theories of well-being to Sen's idea of entitlements and his theory of poverty which requires that a penumbra of potential achievements around each person be measured. The individual is at the center of the scheme, but when the measurements are revealed we discover that, except for the measure of purchasing power, the individual is mainly offstage. The strong focus is on the supporting cast of other people, on the props and machineries, and on those who operate them.

The history of international comparisons is a series of enlarging perspectives on the infrastructure of well-being. From concern about individual access to material goods in general, it goes on to select criteria that will show the level to which personal capabilities can reach. Then political liberties are added, in two stages. This involves constructing a bridge between commodities for private use and quality of life, a bridge consisting of public goods such as roads and sewerage and backed by supporting institutions. Certain measures of justice have been included in the comparisons.

The Human Development Index (HDI) harks back to the International Labour Office statistics for the League of Nations. It was first produced by the United Nations Development Programme (UNDP) in 1990. The inclusion of "human development" in the name of the index shows how much the idea of the good life has gained over old-fashioned comparisons of material welfare and subsistence levels. Subsequent annual editions of the HDI have amended the original concept, but the central idea has remained the same. National income figures hide the distribution of income in a country and do not give much other important information. To provide a comparison of human development involves studying the "enabling environment" in which people can "enjoy long, healthy, and creative lives." The improvement of well-being is the "process of enlarging people's choices" (UNDP 1990: 9).

The three selected influences on choices are life expectancy, education, and access to resources needed for "a decent standard of living" (UNDP 1990: 10). Three additional factors are political freedom, guaranteed human rights, and personal self-respect. Briefly, the concept of human development is "a participatory and dynamic process" that works on two levels: widening people's choices and achieving well-being. Persons with good health, education, and the expectation of a long life also need the opportunity to use their acquired capabilities. For example, they need the opportunity to be active in political organization, take part in social life, and so on.

Three indicators are used for this information: life expectancy at birth, literacy rates, and purchasing-power adjusted gross domestic product (GDP) per capita (in logarithmic form) (UNDP 1990: 12). The first two indicators express the supporting infrastructure on which the individual's life unfolds. Life expectancy, a good indicator of public health, results from commodities such as clean water, capital investment in sewerage, medical practice, and nutritional status. Literacy is a good indicator of the spread of education and access to information. Personal purchasing power (PPP) indicates the individual's prospects for acquiring the good things.

The UNDP arrives at the HDI via a human-deprivation index. This index measures the relative deprivation of individual countries on an ordinal continuum, where maximum deprivation is equal to 1 and minimum deprivation, the target of development, is set at 0. The lowest expectancy of life after birth in 1987 was forty-two years, in Afghanistan, Ethiopia, and Sierra Leone. Somalia's 12 percent provided the lowest literacy rate. Zaire had the minimum PPP-adjusted GDP, $220 per capita. These values represented 1 on the human-deprivation continuum.

At the other end of the scale the target values for each indicator were obtained in the same way. For life expectancy at birth, Japan set the target, with seventy-eight years. The value for literacy was set at 100 percent. The target income was taken from average poverty-line figures of nine industrialized countries: Australia, Canada, Germany, the Netherlands, Norway, Sweden, Switzerland, the United Kingdom, and the United States.

The UNDP ranks individual countries on the human-deprivation continuum for each indicator and then averages the three indicators to come up with the overall deprivation index. The HDI was obtained by subtracting the deprivation index from 1. The outcomes, as shown in Table 3, are extraordinarily interesting. The disparity of incomes among countries goes far beyond differences in HDIs, so, lest this encourage complacency, other information is added. For example, rapidly growing less-developed countries, such as Brazil, have been less than successful in controlling gross human deprivations. Similarly, the inability of rich industrialized countries to halt homelessness, the spread of AIDS, and growing illegal drug use bring home the point that high national income does not mean that human deprivation will be eliminated. It brings its own train of ills.

The annual balance sheets between progress and deprivation are ingeniously drawn up. On nutrition, for example, in 1992, "Daily caloric intake is now about 110% of the overall require-

TABLE 3. THE HUMAN DEVELOPMENT INDEX
FOR INDIVIDUAL COUNTRIES

Balance Sheet of Human Development—Developing Countries

Progress	*Deprivation*
Life expectancy	
• Average life expectancy increased by more than one-third between 1960 and 1990–and is now at 63 years	• 10 million older children and young adults and 14 million young children die each year, most of them from preventable causes
Health	
• The proportion of people with access to health services has risen to 63 percent	• 1.5 billion people still lack basic health care • More than 1.5 billion people do not have safe water, and more than 2 billion lack safe sanitation
Education	
• Adult literacy rates increased between 1970 and 1985, from 46 percent to 60 percent	• More than 1 billion adults are still illiterate • 300 million children are not in primary or secondary school
Income	
• Income per capita grew in the 1980s by almost 4 percent to 9 percent in East Asia • More than one person in four in the 1980s lived in countries with growth rates above 5 percent	• More than 1 billion people still live in absolute poverty • Income per capita has declined over the past decade in Latin America and Sub-Saharan Africa
Children	
• Under-five mortality rates were halved over the past three decades • Immunization coverage for one-year-olds increased dramatically during the 1980s, saving an estimated 1.5 million lives annually	• More than 14 million children die each year before reaching their fifth birthday • 180 million children under five suffer from serious malnutrition

TABLE 3 *(continued)*

Balance Sheet of Human Development—Developing Countries

Progress	*Deprivation*

Women

- Primary-school enrollment for girls increased between 1960 and 1988 from 79 percent to 87 percent
- Women's enrollment in tertiary education has increased almost everywhere—and achieved near-equality with men in Latin America and the Caribbean

- Half of all rural women over 15 are illiterate
- Women are often denied the right to decide whether or when to have children; half a million women die each year from causes related to pregnancy or childbirth
- Women are often legally (or effectively) denied the right to own, inherit, or control property

Rural and urban areas

- The proportion of people living in rural areas with access to adequate sanitation has doubled over the past decade
- 88 percent of urban dwellers have access to health care, and 81 percent have access to safe water

- Only 44 percent of the rural population has access to health care
- There are 2.4 people per habitable room, three times the average in the North. One urban dweller in five miles lives in the nation's largest city

Balance Sheet of Human Development—Industrial Countries

Progress	*Deprivation*

Life expectancy and health

- Average life expectancy is 75 years
- Virtually all births are attended by health personnel, and the maternal mortality rate is only 24 per 100,000 live births
- On average, 8.3 percent of GNP is spent on health care

- Adults on average smoke 1,800 cigarettes per year and consume 4 liters of pure alcohol
- More than half the people born today are likely to die of circulatory and respiratory diseases, many of which will be closely linked to sedentary lifestyles, fat-rich diets, alcohol consumption, and cigarette smoking
- The United States alone reported 137,000 cases of AIDS in 1989

TABLE 3 *(continued)*

Balance Sheet of Human Development—Industrial Countries

Progress	*Deprivation*
Education	
• Governments provide on average 9 years of full-time compulsory education • More than one-third of all graduates are science students • On average, 6 percent of GNP is spent on education	• Almost four persons in ten lack any upper secondary-school education • Only 15 percent of the youth in the age group 20–24 enroll for full-time tertiary education
Income and employment	
• GNP per capita increased between 1976 and 1988 from $4, 850 to $12,510 • Industrial countries produce 85 percent of the global wealth every year	• The wealthiest 20 percent of the population receive almost seven times as much as the poorest 20 percent • About 6.5 percent of the total labor force is unemployed, one-third of it for more than 12 months
Social security	
• Social-welfare expenditures now account on average for 11 percent of GDP	• About 10 million people lived below the poverty level in 1990 (200 million if the USSR and Eastern Europe are included)
Women	
• As many women as men are now enrolled in secondary and tertiary education • Females above the age of 25 have already received, on average, 9 years of schooling • One-fourth of the female graduates are science students	• Women's wages are still only two-thirds of men's wages • There are 50 reported rapes per year per 100,000 females aged 15–59 • Only one-fifth of the parliamentary representatives are women

TABLE 3 *(continued)*

Balance Sheet of Human Development—Industrial Countries

Progress	*Deprivation*
Social fabric	
• People have an opportunity to be informed and connected with one another; there is one radio for every person, one television set and one telephone for every two people • The average family owns a car • Every third person purchases a daily newspaper • There are six library books per person	• Many industrial countries are experiencing rapid change in their social fabric. Most striking examples: Finland, the proportion of single-parent homes (10 percent); Sweden, the highest illegitimacy ratio (42 percent); United States, the highest divorce rate (8 percent) • About 433 persons out of every 100,000 are seriously injured every year in road accidents
Population and environment	
• The current annual population growth rate is around 0.5 percent • Almost the entire population has access to safe water and sanitation facilities	• The dependency ratio is as high as 50 percent • Annual emissions of traditional air pollutants is 42 kilograms per 100 people • The greenhouse index reached 3.5 by 1989

SOURCE: United Nations Development Programme 1991: 24–25.

ment (compared with 90% some 25 years ago)," but "Over 100 million people were affected by famine in 1990. More than a quarter of the world's people do not get enough food, and nearly one billion go hungry" (UNDP 1990: 24).

The development of this index is a great achievement. It is a highly sophisticated attempt to assess the infrastructure of an individual's life. The individual person is not left swinging in midair, without support or clues to what might realistically be possible at that time or place. A person's chances of schooling, nutrition, life expectancy, and income say much more about well-being than do straight comparisons of income, and they do more than merely supply us with answers to questions about individual happiness.

LIVING IS A PRODUCTION PROCESS

The HDI uses what can be measured as clues to how much of his or her potential an individual will be able to achieve. Infrastructure means nothing without supporting institutions. This follows Sen's lead in emphasizing "positive freedom," the freedom to achieve and fulfill a personal potential. The next stage in the history of the idea of well-being was to include the "negative freedoms" in the assessment, which means incorporating political conditions.

Partha Dasgupta starts with the dictum that there is "no one type of freedom that is real freedom" (1993: 42), but he finds the HDI an inadequate measure of well-being because it neglects negative freedoms, freedoms from interference. There has to be a balance between the two freedoms, because if the state is limited to securing negative freedoms, "A person dying of starvation may well be negatively free; but the foreclosure on his freedom to do anything is terminal" (p. 42). Consequently, Dasgupta looks for a concept of welfare that will incorporate both freedoms.

In poor countries individual well-being is often forfeited for the well-being of institutions (Dasgupta 1993: 58). (We would argue that this is true for more than just poor countries.) Norms such as female circumcision in Africa or expectations that women or the old should place their own well-being, or even their survival, after that of their family are internalized to such an extent that the liberal criteria of injustice are not applicable: These people neither are forced nor do they necessarily dislike their social responsibilities. Well-being is not necessarily synonymous with fulfillment of private desires.

Though Sen does not say as much, his concept of well-being treats the activities and achievements of individuals as if they were outputs from some production process that provides the necessary conditions—public health, education, and so forth. Dasgupta reckons that the individual's achievements should be counted as further inputs. This breaks the conventional distinction between producer and consumer: The consumer is also a producer, because living is productive—and we can add that fair institutions are the output. In Dasgupta's model of well-being the whole of human life is a complex production process that calls for inputs and produces outputs that themselves influence the next stage of input.

He starts with the obvious inputs, the commodities that humans consume. At the most basic level these are food, water, shelter, and so forth, which are indicated by "crude measures of commodity availability" (Dasgupta 1993: 38). Those in the physiological production process are transformed into individual functionings, such as survival, health, and the exercise of skills. Outputs are aggregate welfare and "the extent to which certain real, vital interests of persons are being served and promoted" (p. 39). The outcomes of social interaction include positive freedoms. For this reason, Dasgupta includes "background conditions" in his model. These are the political and civil liberties to which an individual has access in a given society.

Dasgupta's three broad indicators of well-being include the individual's current and prospective real income, including non-marketable goods. Take income per capita (GDP), life expectancy at birth, infant survival rate, and adult literacy rate: Income he counts as the input vector of the human productive process, whereas the other three measures are outputs of this process. The idea of positive freedom that is so prominent in Sen's thinking is here treated as a product of the way people have formed their institutions for living together. So far Dasgupta is not doing anything very different from the HDI.

The novelty is to combine these four measures with something to indicate the presence of civil liberties; that is, something to indicate the presence of negative freedom, freedom from arbitrary interference. He wants to find measures of the extent to which citizens can take part in the decision about who governs and by what laws and of the freedoms an individual enjoys vis-à-vis the state, such as freedom of speech and independence of the judiciary (Dasgupta 1993: 109). These two negative freedoms indicate the social institutions that confer value on commodities, allocate them fairly or unfairly, and permit their peaceful and safe enjoyment (p. 37).

Dasgupta has explicitly shifted the focus of research on well-being from the individual to the social mechanisms of allocation—a major advance. The collective process of transforming commodities into well-being (Dasgupta 1993: 44) is a long way from a list of commodities that are supposed to satisfy the individual's basic needs. Dasgupta ingeniously confronts the philosophical difficulties that beset most welfare theories by making full use of the idea of "background" and of the concept of an "enabling environment."

Here is how the tool-to-theory heuristic worked for international comparisons. First there was a conversation from utility-theory assumptions about international comparisons, and then work started on the tool. The tool itself produced dissatisfactions about how it was achieving what it was designed to achieve: comparisons of welfare. So Sen and his colleagues shifted the tool's scope from utilitarian individualism to the infrastructures provided by society. Though Sen's method is formally concerned with the individual, with his idea of positive freedom, he has introduced a concept of social capital. His work with the HDI has shown a method for measuring it. For Sen the infrastructure (education, transport, communications, public health, or whatever one cares to measure) gives the individual a supporting environment of opportunity for self-realization. Dasgupta adds another set of background conditions to indicate freedom from arbitrary despoilment and misrule. In each case the individual is nominally to the fore and the rest of society to the rear. But only nominally, for the measures are designed to assess the institutional support for the individual.

CRITICISM

But even now there is scope for criticism of the chosen indicators. First, a social being's essential need, on which everything else depends, even food and shelter, is communication. The infrastructure of communication is not emphasized enough. Consider literacy, for example: Does not this measure need to be updated? What about numeracy? Computer competence could be added too, for it is clear that the absence of facilities and training puts a severe limit on the individual's capabilities and functioning. The ratio of telephones to population, and of personal computers and electronic communication, will show how much inhabitants of poor countries are at a lower level of communication with each other and are, de facto, excluded from communication with the rich. The distribution of communication technology sums up the meaning of the other indexes of well-being (Douglas and Isherwood 1979).

Second, indicators have been chosen to measure liberty and justice, but we foresee that these measures will eventually be improved. The measures in use seem fair enough. Liberty and justice are the topics on which social beings disagree most deeply and systematically. But even though they be honored and practiced, there will still be furious disputes about historical injustice—for example, about appropriation of land and dispossession or about rights of immigrants, questions which it would be wrong to dismiss as political. Individual welfare will suffer in a country that is violently disturbed and on the brink of civil war.

CHAPTER FOUR

For a Concept
of the Whole Person

The microcosm's control over our minds is elusive. You have to lay traps to catch it at work. One of the traps is to recognize it as a feedback system, for this allows it to be caught at a number of different points. In chapter 3 we described *Homo œconomicus* as exemplifying a tools-to-theory model. The feedback part of the story is that the favored institutional form generates its own favored version of workable knowledge and that the knowledge generates the approved testing processes, proofs, and justifications that protect it. It creates among the users of the knowledge a vested interest in its present form, and, most stifling of all, it instills suspicion of alternatives. To counteract it our strategy must be crude and direct. You must be able to see what we are doing. First we will show the disadvantages to social theory of bundling out of sight the rich diversity of persons; then we will suggest a way of identifying them. After that, we will retrace our steps and explain the advantages for welfare policy of recognizing their peculiarities.

RATIONALITY

At present the individual who is so central to our social thought is a little universe complete unto itself. The psyche is the frame onto which the operations of rational choice are pegged. Like a set of Chinese boxes, specific functions, reason and emotion, benevolence and self-interest, reign each in its own sphere and contend each with the other, like homunculi whose tugs-of-war replicate the final choices of the sovereign person. Everything that results in choice goes on inside the psyche. It has been stripped down precisely to get away from metaphysical doctrines that are tied to particular religions or interests.

In the eighteenth century Catholics, Protestants, and atheists realized that they had to talk to each other. It was hardly globalization as we are experiencing it, but there was a similar bracing challenge to discard outworn, divisive ideologies. The Thirty Years' War had demonstrated how deeply and cruelly Christianity could divide: There was no unifying philosophy to which Italians, French, and Germans could subscribe, as well as the Scottish and English. The idea of human rationality was promoted for this task. Rationality, already the guarantor of the new science, seemed to be a principle noble enough to engage loyalty and comprehensive and dynamic enough to stand on its own. The individual's innate capacity for logic and a very spare list of basic sentiments were all that was needed. Like a Protestant reading of the Bible, under God's direct guidance without distortion from mediating institutions, objectivity became the guiding principle of rational inquiry.

It was to have been a tool to detect and expose ideology, but sooner or later the project acquired ideology of its own. In effect, when it comes to talking about human behavior, objectivity is

equally difficult, with or without ideological guidelines. Historically it has been assumed that there will be a conflict of interest
between individual claims and those of the community, and this
conflict has often been the focus of political alignment. It is obvious that a theory of law and politics that starts and ends with
individual happiness is not going to stay neutral in that debate.
There is going to be a great deal of moralizing, and moralizing
puts objectivity in jeopardy.

That ground has been well tilled already. Take, for example, a
favorite neutral term of economic justification, *efficiency*. Not neutral at all when used in the language of political affray, it relates
ends to means without waste, but its contrast set, inefficiency,
is wasteful, and who can justify wastefulness? The term is so laden
that in any court a case against efficiency is doomed to be
dismissed as traditionalist, obscurantist, confused, sentimental.
When rhetoric has descended to this level the argument ought to
shift from how most efficiently to achieve agreed ends to the value
of the ends proposed. What is good? What is the good society?

The liberal philosopher forbears to answer except in terms
that relate to the well-being of a standard representative individual. Forbearing to answer comes close to forbearing to think.
The microcosm is jealous of ways of thinking about values that
preempt the individual's private judgment. We have to find ways
of talking about choice and preference without criticizing anyone
else's preference or cultural bias. The tempting solution is to
avoid politics and look for explanations of human behavior inside
the individual person. The model of economic man serves this
purpose well, for several things can be said about his preferences:
Other things being equal, he will prefer more, rather than less, of

something he wants, and his wants are ordered. He points the way toward a universal logic of preferences.

A UNIVERSAL LOGIC

In some branches of cognitive psychology a lot of energy goes into either searching for a universal logic or delimiting where the authority of rational-choice theory runs. For example, Daniel Kahneman and Amos Tversky (1981) find it a universal principle that individuals generally treat losses and gains asymmetrically. People are reported to be much more unhappy at the thought of a loss than happy at the thought of a gain. According to Kahneman, the principle of asymmetric losses and gains is founded in biological origins (Kahneman 1993). Loss aversion is rooted in the deep asymmetry between pain and pleasure, which in turn is rooted in a necessary asymmetry between two biologically significant commands, "Desist" and "Proceed," in its turn rooted in neurological signaling of pain and pleasure. In one move the cognitive psychologists have served the microcosm by harnessing biology to the support of the hedonic calculus.

Of course, there are problems with this alleged universal principle. First, recognition of a loss is a more complex process than recognizing pain. Second, the assumption that humans come to financial or any other decisions uninfluenced by the culture in which they live is counterintuitive. Third, the central thesis that culture can be disregarded is self-validating, because the method of inquiry makes a great effort to eliminate cultural differences. The subjects of the experiments are carefully homogenized in the name of objectivity.

The argument starts from a supposed principle of rational choice. If equivalent gains and losses are considered to be events of exactly the same kind, with just a difference of a plus or minus, they ought to provoke equivalent reactions. That this is not so is shown by responses to hypothetical examples in questionnaires. It turns out that people "are more sensitive to out-of-pocket costs than to opportunity costs and more sensitive to losses than to foregone gains" (Kahneman and Tversky 1981: 731). When responding to questions that have been carefully drafted to exclude extraneous bias-introducing information, the subjects of these experiments answer with striking near-unanimity.

The question is whether it is unfair to reduce a rate of reward that has been entered into a person's regular expectations.

Question A.

A small photocopying shop has an employee who has worked in the shop for six months and earns $9 an hour. Business continues to be satisfactory, but a factory in the area has closed and unemployment has increased. Other small shops have now hired reliable workers at $7 an hour to perform jobs similar to those done by the photocopy shop employee. The owner of the photocopying shop reduces the employee's wage to $7.

(N = 98) Acceptable 17%; Unfair 83%

Question B.

A small photocopying shop has one employee . . . (as in Question A). . . . The current employee leaves, and the owner decides to pay a replacement $7 an hour.

(N = 125) Acceptable 73%; Unfair 27%

(Kahneman, Knetsch, and Thaler 1986)

If this is a discovery about regularly predictable attitudes to losses and gains, it would have tremendous implications for market psychology. If he is expected to make rational choices, the employer would reduce loss by passing it on to consumers, or employees, or however he can. But the answers to the question about justice of imposed losses run against the expectation. The answers in favor of the employer's accepting a loss rather than passing it on would quickly bring the economy to a standstill if the sentiment behind them were indeed universal.

However, the fictive case is not analyzed: The implicit principle followed by the majority of respondents is that the employer has a responsibility to maintain his initial bargain with the employee forever, regardless of loss and inconvenience to himself. But surely this value varies in different cultures. The respondents are indignant that someone should cause another to suffer a loss. Does it help objectivity to cut out information about them? Who are they? If they are young, unemployed, or immigrants, or all academics in tenured jobs, we would suspect them of identifying themselves with the hapless employees. What happens when the same question is put to a sample of hard-pressed employers? Are they not supposed also to reject a prospect of loss on their own behalf? Respondents committed to a fully individualized market culture would protect the principle of freely terminable contracts, whereas respondents committed to a hierarchical culture would protect the permanent responsibility of the employer to protect his employees from market hazards.

Our contemporary cognitive psychologists subscribe to something like the eighteenth-century illusion of the feral child. They can get away with it because there is a vacuum. Nothing discredits the naive essentialism because there is no theory of the person as a social being, solidary with like-minded others and collectively hostile to deviant others. Prospects of loss and gain go deep, and the idea is that if we dig deep enough we will reach the true essence of the human rational being. But why should we suppose there is an essence? The enterprise is based on the onion-skin image of the person: Strip off layer after layer of coverings added fortuitously by life's experiences, and at the bottom you will come to the true essence of personhood, a rational being with universal human proclivities. But this rational being is not equipped with emotions—or, rather, we might say that the rationality of *Homo œconomicus* is being considered apart from emotion.

ENVY, FRUSTRATION, AND OTHER EMOTIONS

In the beginning of the modern period emotion became known as the enemy of rational processes rather than as their ally. A strong account of rationality without an equally well-worked-out account of psychology has led emotion to be treated as an explanation for why behavior diverges from the rational norm. In various branches of the social sciences the workings of reason are studied without reference to subjectivity. There is no reason why this practice should not have useful results. For example, sociobiology derives a new analytical approach from the idea of individual competitive self-interest. The simple idea of rational calculation attributed to the gene explains the behavior of primates and other mammals (Dunbar 1989). This approach undoubtedly owes some of its explanatory power to its compatibility with the dominant paradigm of rationality.

Most of the formal practice of psychology is centered in professions of pure experiment or of therapy. It is not surprising that between these professions there is no agreed synthesis about human cognition or human emotion. In default of a theory, the social sciences have generally tried to circumvent questions that have to be answered by reference to individual feelings. Objectivity would require no less. But the demands of objectivity are unrealistically austere. To evade objectivity's strictures it is tempting to delve into our own everyday feelings and produce talk that others think they understand because of their access to similar resources. Western social thinkers have acquired a habit of buttressing their arguments with ad hoc scraps of psychology from personal experience or from literature and the arts.

To an anthropologist it is surprising—indeed, to anyone who expects objectivity it is surprising. Here are famous scholars, writing about social justice in the usual liberal posture of respect for objectivity. Then suddenly, without an apology or a by your leave, when stuck for an explanation they produce a new kind of virtue or a new form of mental aberration to explain why people are doing what they do.

Contemporary treatises on social justice contain homilies on envy. An eminent philosopher who solemnly identifies envy goes on to distinguish between "reasonable envy," "excusable envy," and "excessive envy" (Rawls 1971). Other philosophers who carefully distinguish envy from jealousy and resentment (Nozick 1974) or who find the mathematical formula for representing social justice in terms of obviating resentment (Varian 1974) are ostensibly not doing so in order to import moral judgments.

In risk research the word *fear* is bandied about as if it had independent standing, as is the word *dread*. These are references to emotional states for which the only evidence is verbal, and no distinction is made between verbal evidence received at the psychoanalyst's couch or the headlines about a media event.

Some of the references to emotions are in the spirit of attempting to bring to attention hitherto insufficiently recognized psychological propensities. Albert Hirschman offers a subtle analysis of attitudes toward economic development in which he suggests that "the general human disposition to be disappointed has hidden from view the fact that there are important *variations* in the incidence and intensity of disappointment at different times and in relation to different activities and commodities" (Hirschman 1981: 12). He wants a place for disappointment in the list of human motivations and inhibitions, but where can he find such a list? Jon Elster introduces frustration in the same vein: "the classical finding from *The American Soldier* that there was a positive correlation between possibilities of promotion and level of frustration over the promotion system" (Elster 1982: 225).

Anthropology must register objections to random reliance on psychological variables and covert jumps between levels of verbal usage. At one level, psychology is a professional practice and theory. The professionals have their own agenda and canons of criticism, related to a distinctive field of practice. Their terminology gives justification for therapies, for judicial decisions about sanity, for theories of child development in education. The output of the discipline is in treatises and textbooks and student dissertations.

At another level, it is psychology that emerges in contexts of action and dispute. We hear its voice speaking informally in therapy consultations and in tribunals, or families, or schools—for example, about disciplining children or reproaching parents. This is folk psychology: It provides a constantly changing version of the human being, a folk model of the person which is the self-perception of a community. Norms are issued from both levels. It is not at all the context for objectivity and impartial distance. When philosophers attribute behavior to envy they are only invoking a folk model—their own. Even if they do not intend to use it in that way, the words come out of the vocabulary of blame and coercion. The words are being paraded in analytical sentences as if they had a technical meaning. But in each folk community in which blaming and exonerating go on, the values of virtue and vice shift from one generation to the next. In the learned context the usage is bogus: It means nothing. It is inadmissible to use the language of pinning responsibility as if it were neutral to moral judgments.

Take the case of a doctor's diagnosis. Inevitably, in the tension and anxiety of sickness, the nature of responsibility is thrashed out, and so also, inevitably, is the conception of the person. The doctor is pushed to pronounce on causes. Friends may ask whether the damage to the body is self-inflicted by neglect or ignorance or whether some other person is responsible. A claim for damages may arise. The practitioner may try to avoid the issue of blame by a no-fault diagnosis, but conflict may be too strong for a natural-causes verdict. In courts of law the judges cannot avoid drawing on an implicit notion of the person. Where social life is organized, the inquirer will find an organized folk psychology in place (Heelas and Locke 1981).

Folk theories about the psyche emerge in a discourse of confrontation. Emotions credited to a person are potential weapons of abuse and disparagement. Folk psychologizing is a powerful strategy of rejection because it diminishes the opponent's claims to rationality. One effect of folk psychology is to keep marginalized sectors of the community in the margins. Feminist sociology has shown how emotional unbalance has been used to disqualify women from positions of responsibility (Ardener 1975). Techniques of exclusion by disparagement have been studied in English social anthropology since the 1930s (Evans-Pritchard 1937). It has become much more famous since the 1970s through the powerful writings of Michel Foucault on hospitals, asylums, and the body as the subject of social disciplining. Ethnomethodology has made this theme its own, by its elaborate critique of imputed motives (Burke 1950). Motives and emotions also have to be explained.

XENOPHOBIA, DISTRESS, AND LONELINESS

Perhaps the examples we have given are trivial. It may sound like an academic quibble to say that it is not acceptable to use emotions as explanations for behavior. What does it matter if learned jurists refer to emotions that we all can understand? Our case rests precisely on the fact that we can understand references to vanity, indignation, or the spirit of emulation. That is part of the trouble. We understand the disparagement because we share the bias. For example, moral condemnation of good things wasted on self-display is a criticism made by the established elite; there is nothing objective whatsoever in its contempt for the pretensions of the new rich.

Some learned appeals to the emotions are not disparagements but calls for sympathy and action. A nontrivial contemporary example is the weight carried by the ideas of fear and dread in studies of the perception of risk. Crisis theory, stress theory, and deprivation theory are all variants of explanation by reference to emotions, and they are equally unsatisfactory.

The argument is implicitly ad hominem: A sect expresses anger, and if you were marginalized like that, you would feel anger too; a protesting mob is violent, and if you were as impoverished as the rioters, you would feel violent too; an ecstatic religion provides competition for the staid rites of an established church, but if you were disappointed, wouldn't you too seek compensation in states of dissociation? In the absence of a theory of the person and the absence of a theory of emotion, the appeal to empathy is a nonexplanation. This did not matter when it was only a habit of historians who were reflecting on the past. But now there are major movements, variously called fundamentalism, sectarianism, revivalism, or radical extremism, which can never be understood in these terms. The language of emotions obscures what is happening. Or you could say that the language of the hustings and the pulpit has replaced that of the social sciences.

First, the idea that religious dissent is religious deviance betrays a prejudice. The agenda is set so that nothing needs to be explained about religious behavior of the conventionally devout. Only the behavior of protesting sects is out of line; and it is also implied that established religions are less coercive. Implicitly sectarian behavior deserves special study when it directs violence against the establishment. The distorting bias can be corrected only by setting the protagonists in religious disputes on the same footing.

But why are we talking about religious dissent instead of about dissenting minorities in general? A second weakness is to put religious history and religious sociology behind a fence. This is clearly unrealistic: Any dissenting movement can turn into a religious one if it decides to escalate its claims by invoking a special mission from God; and, conversely, religious dissent often espouses a social program.

Separating the two fields puts explanations of religion into a different compartment, one in which ordinary weekday sociological and political explanations do not apply. Emotions are all that are left as explanatory factors. Instead of argument we read pious hope and respectful sympathy for private disappointment and frustration.

Nobody now would see ecstatic religions quite so crudely as responses to political oppression as did V. Horio Lanternari (1960). No one would probably be so naive as to explain them as wish-fulfilling deviations from normal religion. But even the more nuanced versions of recent religious sociology make similar assumptions. If we were as deprived and exploited, all we affluent rationalists would be as single-minded and devout. So, third, religious movements are supposed to start with the poor, in rural poverty or urban slums. Even though the exact opposite is often the case, the old idea dies hard.

NONHUMAN INTELLIGENCE

There are signs that the ice floe is breaking, for social influences are being considered by cognitive scientists, psychologists as well as anthropologists (Goody 1995). These sources give a fair impression of a science at a transitional stage: ad hoc casting around for social factors to throw into the cooking pot, as if flavoring the stew were the main aim. These social psychologists avoid the rational-choice paradigm and say they would like to build social factors into their model of cognition, but it is difficult to see that they have a model at all. First they would need to work out an account of social factors.

It may be easier for zoologists to work out social factors for primates, not so much because they are complete outsiders looking at the behavior of advanced vertebrates but because they are so far removed from social interaction that they can assume a simple goal, physical survival. It is interesting that in studying animal behavior, too, the eye of the researcher has been constrained by old assumptions about rigid species-specific patterns. Questions such as "Why are they mating in this pattern?" or "Why do they go in big herds?" used to be answered by reference to some species-friendly evolutionary principle of action found in the genetically transmitted psyche of the animal itself: its instincts. It suggests that the meme that protects the *Homo œconomicus* paradigm does not like to think that nonhumans exercise rational choice.

However, ethologists have come a long way. We used to think that animals could not form concepts or classify or plan ahead to reach goals. Now we know better.

It turns out that the internal dynamics of complex animal societies which used to be left blank yield to analysis in terms of intelligent, individual responses to external influences. In "Social Systems as Optimal Strategy Sets: The Costs and Benefits of Sociality," Robin Dunbar (1989) shows how to use the rational-choice paradigm to explain social behavior and to shed new light on animal cognition. For example, if gelada and hamadryas baboons vary the size of their social units consistently to make a better trade-off between predation risks and exploitation of grassland resources, there must be some thinking going on.

Similar cost-benefit and rational-choice strategies explain patterns of mating and other social behaviors.

This is what we had in mind in chapter 3 when we asked why the whole rational-choice tool kit should be thrown out. Whether the form of society is treated as a means to a goal, as the nonhuman primates just cited use it as a means to survival, or as a goal in itself, the same analytical tools can be used to discover the efficient means. So if a large, complex social system is accepted as a goal by the members of a community, there are certain practices which would be nonproductive for that goal. If a social system of individual foragers is the goal, there are other social practices which would be nonproductive for that goal. And among the questions that would be asked, of ourselves as well as of the nonhuman primates, is what sort of advantages for individuals does one social system have as against another, and what kind of external environmental constraints indicate one system or another as more or as less fitting?

ARTICULATING THE CONCEPT OF THE WHOLE PERSON

One criticism of the present state of the art would really hurt: to accuse it of lacking objectivity. But this is valid. An unarticulated concept of the person excuses ad hoc psychic inventions such as we have been describing, or it allows political advocacy to be pursued in hidden ways.

There is no denying that the philosophers of the West have had good reasons for keeping the person as a taboo area that can be talked about but not systematized. We have had a bad experience with dictators and religions using their definitions of what the human person needs (Douglas 1992b). One result of that bad experience is our wish to put important, sensitive topics outside the scope of political conflict. For these reasons the mind is stripped bare and plunged naked into the statistical cauldron, while influences from other minds are systematically cauterized. So we are left with the paradox that the social sciences' description of the self does not refer to a social being. As the microcosm requires, everything has to be sacrificed to generality, which is expected to protect objectivity, but the generality tends to evacuate meaning. Until the gap that is the empty self is filled, most of the other gaps in the social sciences will generate inscrutable paradoxes.

The history of the Anglo-Saxon social sciences requires that any new ways of describing the self must be empirical, scientistic, and parsimonious. They must not be either mystical or biased. We need an all-purpose, minimal model of the person, first as rational and capable of ordering preferences consistently, of having goals and intentions for reaching them. As a social being the person needs to be capable of reading messages from other persons, of responding to these and of composing intelligible messages to send out. This requires some even more basic qualities: The person has to have beliefs about how the world is and how it works, ontological knowledge, and knowledge about how other persons behave, which Max Weber (1949: 174) called "nomological" (knowledge of empirically found rules about how human beings are prone to behave under given situations). Equipped with the wherewithal to make choices, the rational social being will apply choice to dealings with other persons and will develop strategies for manipulating and controlling them and for escaping unwanted control.

Here we have the beginnings of a social model of the self. It closely resembles Daniel Dennett's model of the person, which he developed to bridge various sciences dealing with mind, artificial intelligence, games theory, psychology, and philosophy. In his all-purpose, minimal model the person starts as an "intentional system." For Dennett's theoretical purposes, persons are rational beings whose actions can be understood in terms of their intentions, and these can be construed from the logical relations between their beliefs and desires. His intentional system has three conditions: rationality, intentions, and a reciprocal stance toward and from other intentional systems. "Intentionality" is the capability to have intentions that persons ascribe to each other. A person who takes an "intentional stance" expects to be able to predict how other persons are going to behave and makes this knowledge the basis for strategies in fulfilling intended goals (Dennett 1987).

So far, so good. What would have been, not so long ago, an unusual merit of this abstract model is that it makes interaction with other persons the prime activity of a person. In other words, this being is inherently social. Intentional systems are watching each other and interpreting each other's intentions, anticipating and responding. Far from being a lone prophet, cognitive scientists are writing social interaction into the account of the individual's mind from the beginning. Babies are thought to be equipped with the capacity to develop theories of mind, and the size and complexity of the brain testify to the intellectual powers that are stimulated by living in community. (For a popular summary, see Dunbar 1995, chap. 7, "The Social Brain.")

In spite of its merits, Dennett's model has the same grave flaw as do other social science models of the person. Because it says nothing about culture, we are still contemplating the feral child, still thinking about a tabula rasa on which everything is to be drawn from scratch, still scrabbling inside the onion skin for an essential element. Without making space for culture, the model is vacuous. Culture is the result of people getting together; it is the result of mutual encouragement and coercion. Culture is the selective screen through which the individual receives knowledge of how the world works and how people behave. For humans nothing is known from scratch, everything is transmitted through other persons, and they are not isolated influences. In banding together they have contrived a coding device for acceptable knowledge. So well hidden is the coding that any true knowledge claims to be independent of history and cultural bias. The search for authenticity and authority ends with the construction of a macrocosm of God or nature to which the new items of knowledge must conform.

There are several ways to advance a social model of mind that will circumvent the jealous microcosm. One would be to build into it a general social intention. We want to understand better the springs of sociality. It might be enough to include the idea that the social being has an open set of intentions about how to live together with other social beings. We would not have to specify what the content of the set would be; it would be enough to call it a basic constitution-framing capacity. Some people like to live in an intimate huddle, some at a discreet distance; some like to be regimented, others like to boss. Their constitutional preferences will govern their judgments of other people's intentions. Having gone so far, the next step would be to incorporate only viable social arrangements into the model, only constitutions that have a chance of working. This move would allow us to write culture into a feedback cycle, as follows.

For each form of stable organization there would be a range of values and theories about persons' behavior and about the world adapted to it. The little embryonic person starting to acquire knowledge inside one of these cultural systems would be developing tastes and habits and constitutional preferences. The other persons in this learning environment would be applying the rewards and penalties that correspond to their constitutional preferences. The outside environment would prove something about the practical viability of their choices in the prevailing conditions. The cultural filter would sift all incoming information. The organization recruiting and training its personnel to suit the external conditions would be enjoying positive feedback and bowling along on a path of greater institutional specialization. In a short time a complex system of positions would be well established, or egalitarianism, or patron-client individualism. The model would have as many kinds of cultural persons as kinds of stable organizations. And one of its merits would be its ability to incorporate varieties of political preferences in the makeup of persons.

PERSONAL CHOICE

It would be a mistake to stop the development of the model at this point. Nowhere have we said that a person cannot change his or her set of intentions or that an organization cannot change its character. Such rigidity would be a liability for our scheme. The person survives by being sensitive to the pressures of others, continuously engaged in responding and looking for response from other persons, new persons can arrive, outside conditions can change. By banding together, the dissidents can make their organization shift or let in new ideas. There is no reason to suppose that a person cannot adapt to any form of organization, exchange an old set of intentions for new ones, change and develop; the model needs to allow for transformation through social interaction.

The theory of culture over the last two decades has come to see cultural activity in the form of a lively debate among intelligent beings. At all times any collection of people will be teeming with dissension. However small the group, some members will favor the status quo and tradition, and some will favor change. The community will be tugged this way and that by rival views of how it ought to be organized. The theory works with a heuristic base of four organizational types, each emanating its appropriate cultural bias (this will be explained in chapter 5). Meanwhile, it is a simple step to assume that inside each person are four possible sets of social preferences, corresponding to the options given by the other persons outside. Inside the person these proclivities will strive with each other as persons strive for the best way to organize the community.

In principle the model is now articulated: It is meshed with the social life of others, and they with external conditions. It is dynamic: There is feedback between the influences from other persons and the preferences held by an individual and between both and the world. It is a circle. There is scope for change. The person does not have to be left as an empty cipher about which everything is assumed and nothing is explicit. We have quoted Marilyn Strathern's remark that in Melanesia for "person" one could well write "gift," and her explanation that a person is regarded there as the sum of the transactions achieved (Strathern 1992). The quality of personhood depends on the variety of relationships persons are capable of sustaining with others. Dennett's intentional model, developed as we have suggested, can take into account all the exchanges into which the person enters in the course of a lifetime.

In conclusion, notice several distinct advantages to be drawn from the exercise. One gain is that emotions become more problematic. Both emotion and behavior are parts of a generative system that also produces culture. Studying how this system works cannot be shirked. Emotions were only able to supply explanation when they seemed to be ultimate and beyond explanation themselves. But how can we be content with disappointment or frustration as explanations of the growth of fundamentalism? An explanation of social behavior that creams off a few symptoms and links them to emotions encourages a fatal intellectual failing: lack of curiosity. But this is not a crime. There are generally reasons for not pushing an inquiry too far.

Patches of ignorance are carefully preserved in any social group. A liberal democracy has to work hard on cultivating ignorance so that plural cultures can subsist side by side. Pluralism requires politics to be reduced to a common denominator. That inherently political animals, left to themselves, choose different political machineries to embody their separate aims is one of those dangerous ideas from which the social sciences have been protected. Because political analysis has been kept apart from social and psychological analysis, words for emotions have to do duty for explanation. Yet they are so weighted with discrimination that any learned discussion of justice should scrupulously avoid them. We cannot assume that everyone understands what envy, or frustration, is—as if they were universals.

Michel Foucault will have written in vain if the discourse on bodily and psychic disciplines is not recognized as an instrument of intellectual coercion (Foucault 1980). It is inevitable and right that a concept of the person should be central in a theory of social justice. But, as it happens, the equivalent thing that exists in the theory of rational behavior is an empty cipher; generations have done their best to excise its details. The place is kept empty as a way of safeguarding objectivity.

Because no one else is there, the person is like a cinematic Tarzan, swinging freely from branch to branch before a painted backdrop of forest scenery. Everything around him is unreal; only his wants coming from inside himself are authentic. Frustration must be calmed and disappointment demands redress, all on the model of imperious hunger and thirst, the needs of agricultural land, and the model of the market.

CHAPTER FIVE

Four Whole Persons

Are the missing persons really necessary? Why would it be better for the social sciences to be more integrated? A culture that grows out of practice is to some extent a creature of that practice; if we judge the practice to be good, we should be content to let a few intellectual discrepancies float around.

Persons in all the richness of their political disagreements have been made to disappear. Perhaps it is as necessary for a plural democracy to perform this vanishing trick as it is for other kinds of cultures to go through strange intellectual twists. Searching too hard for coherence at the summit of a thought system may be a waste of time. In our case, the idea of the person is sacred ground. Some vapid talk and tight philosophical tangles may be a small price to pay for protecting individual rights. Even if the metaphysical elements can be put together coherently, would any purpose be served?

Trying to answer those questions involves the ticklish matter of seeing through the veils of our own culture. Is it worth it? Is it possible? In this chapter we will show how it can be done by out-lining a cultural theory that does not diminish a person's politi-cal dignity. The theory will have to be compatible with the dom-inant culture, for it is no good trying to oust that. It will have to be developed for specific problems and to be confined to specific niches of our lives. We then will show how a theory of persons that gives credit for strong moral dissent would improve our understanding of ourselves. It would even have practical value at the policy level.

PARABLES AND FICTIONS

The exercise we are about to embark upon has something in com-mon with certain parables in political philosophy that try to con-front plural doctrines of justice: for example, Bruce Ackerman's (1980) script for a spaceship whose captain applied strict rules of dialogue for a liberal society, the aim being to allow criticism and disagreement without bringing the dialogue to an end; or the more recent essay on justification by Luc Boltanski and Laurent Thévenot (1991), which compares six philosophers' cities or worlds that share principles about common humanity and justice but that develop justification of persons differently. The "world of opinion," for instance, makes reputation, renown, visibility, and distinction the arbiters of differences between persons. The "civic world" makes the collectivity preeminent, and persons are distinguished according to their representative or delegated status. In a "domestic world," persons are distinguished accord-ing to generation, tradition, and internal hierarchies of families. There is also a "commercial world," in which personal status depends on the outcomes of rivalry and competition, as well as an "industrial world," in which persons are judged according to effective power. The authors recognize that these worlds are to some extent mutually dependent and to some extent in competition. Their elucidation of different principles of justification is of great interest.

There are excellent fictional portrayals of different worlds governed by different principles of organization and developing, in consequence, different judgments of merit. A superb example is Thornton Wilder's story (1973) about Newport, Rhode Island, in the 1920s. The narrator is an insufferably conceited young man who, by teaching tennis and languages, penetrates Newport's separate "worlds" or "cities." He thinks of Newport as a modern Troy, built on nine sites. The first city was a seventeenth-century village of which little remained but a few buildings. The second city was the eighteenth-century town that left splendid architecture, books, and other records. The third city was the seaport, now only squalid moorings and a few pleasure boats, the city of the wharfside and of sailors and fishers and others making their livelihood by boats and keeping themselves to themselves. The fourth city was a system of old forts and training bases, now inhabited by men of the naval and military stations and their families, for whom the rest of Newport was out of bounds, so they were a world to themselves. The fifth city was represented by a few intellectuals, who had a scholarly cast of mind and were interested in the second city. The sixth city was that of the vulgar rich, summer visitors who came from New York City to spend annual holidays in their huge "cottages." These transients were exclusive and tried to keep out fortune hunters and parasites; they believed there was nothing that money could not buy, but they continually proved that it was not so by the evidence of their own unhappiness, relished by the disapproving permanent residents. The seventh city, that of the servants of the rich, was hierarchical and traditionalist, as was the ninth city, that of the burghers, who had little to do with the servants except through their powerful ally, the chief of police, who through the narrative intervenes dramatically on the side of law and order. Eighth was the city of the hangers-on, parasites, scroungers, and adventurers, who tried to force their way into the circle of the very rich and were sedulously ejected.

The fictional array of possible worlds in Newport, and the documented real worlds selected by Boltanski and Thévenot, illustrate a common problem. How can the selection be justified? How does the classification escape being arbitrary? Why six cities, or nine? In Wilder's novel, when the hero has confided to a resident his theory of the nine cities of Newport, the latter reflects and then suggests that there are really fifteen. Why not? Nine cities or fifteen? What difference does it make to the novel, which is not pretending to authenticity or ethnographic completeness? The fact that the story has completely left out the very honorable and ancient Jewish community of Newport may not matter. The nine cities have enough verisimilitude for us to enjoy the story. But not enough if we want to solve a problem.

The problem is to determine how many distinct kinds of cities or worlds we need for a theory of cultural bias. The selection must be able to be justified; it must be exhaustive and comprehensive in relation to the problem. The cities should be incompatible with each other, at least insofar as making competing demands on resources; each should be adversarially defined in relation to the others, in the sense that they apply incompatible judgments of personal worth and seek incompatible goals; each should put different factors into its decision-making processes, and so come up with different solutions; each should be interacting with the others, thus sharpening its sense of difference through contrast and conflict.

Relative wealth should not make a difference to the classification of cultures. Wilder has captured the exclusiveness of the city of the servants and the city of the established burghers, their suspicion of newcomers, their common disapproval of the summer visitors' flaunting extravagance and loose sexual mores. Good from the narrative point of view, but bad from the point of view of cultural theory, he has allowed his own bias to organize his material. Between the servants and the burghers on the one hand, whom he respects, and the summer visitors on the other, whom he despises, he is not impartial. He does not have a principle of selection among possible cities that will spread out a representative series of cultural biases. The same for the justificatory worlds of Thévenot and Boltanski: There is no obvious reason why three worlds would not have been enough or why they should stop at six.

CULTURAL BIAS

To identify the significant varieties of culture we line them up systematically according to a fourfold set of biases, each aggressively self-defined against the others (Figure 3). Why four? This is much discussed among anthropologists who try to find the distinctive principles that organize different realms of discourse. The cultural theory on which we are relying in this volume assumes that four types of cultural bias are always potentially

B = isolates, by choice or compulsion, literally alone or isolated in complex structures (eclectic values)	**C** = strongly incorporated groups with complex structure (hierarchies, for example)
A = weak structure, weak incorporation (competitive individualism)	**D** = strongly incorporated groups with weak structure (egalitarian enclaves, or sects, for example)

Figure 3. The cultural map.

present in any group of persons, all four competing with one another and each tipping behavior toward one or another type of organization. Four, not because four types are all that there are, but for the sake of having a parsimonious model of organizations, in two dimensions only.

If anyone protests that there are really fifteen, five hundred, or two thousand types, or six or eight dimensions, they mistake the exercise. Eleven thousand or a million would *not* be enough to cover the variety that is out there. But for explanatory value, three, four, or five types of social environments are enough to generate the three, four, or five cosmologies that serve to stabilize four or five kinds of organization. Michael Thompson (Ellis, Thompson, and Wildavsky 1990) can justify five different cultural biases, whereas Manfred Schmutzer (1994) argues that only four are mathematically possible. According to the "strong program" of the theory, these four are theoretically sufficient because there are only four stable organizational forms—the rest are transitional.

Of four cultural biases, four worlds, four cities—call them what you like—the first (C on the map) supports tradition and order. The second (A) stands for individual competition and holds no brief for tradition for its own sake. These two, obviously adversarial, correspond for all intents and purposes to the Weberian distinction between hierarchies and markets that has worn so well in the social sciences. The third cultural bias (D) corresponds to the closed egalitarian system, a sectarian enclave. It is often but not necessarily religious. The determining feature is the commitment to equality, which usually is maintained by elaborate rules (Rayner and Flanagan 1988) and results in organizational weakness and a bias toward conspiracy theory. The fourth (B) is the option for anyone who avoids alignment and who does not intend to lead or persuade or organize; keeping apart from the struggle produces the bias toward isolation and fatalism.

These four cultures are discriminated on principles of organization. The top half of the diagram is a society dominated by a grid of compartments, fixed positions, and separating rules that restrict individual free choice. The grid is progressively weakened going downward. From left to right the individuals start alone or independently and are progressively organized into bounded groups. The top right gives you a complexly ordered collectivity; the bottom right gives you a simple egalitarian collectivity. On the bottom left, where collective action is weak, individuals negotiate with each other freely: That is the ideal for rational economic man. In the top left, individuals are more constrained than elsewhere by separating rules or economic hindrances.

The map is a template from which the four cultures can be constructed. In view of the variety of ways of organizing, one should be curious about what values are necessary for one pattern rather than another to be supported. Each culture is good for different organizational purposes. When a complex coordination has advantages, it makes sense to develop the top right pattern and to cultivate the values and attitudes that justify it. When individual initiative is needed, it makes sense to develop the bottom left pattern and the values that go with it. When concerted protest is needed, it makes sense to sink individual differences and go for the egalitarian group. And so on.

In this scheme each city, world, or cultural type is defined in opposition to the others and recruits its supporters or loses them competitively. It is no accident that any word you may choose for labeling these four opposed cultures evokes bias, if it is not actually seen as pejorative. For some, complexity is a bad word, market is pejorative for others, sect is dismissive, fatalist is derisive. So they were originally named A, B, C, D, after the two dimensions on which the model was constructed: structure (in the vertical dimension) and incorporation (in the horizontal).

The two most familiar cultures are opposed on the map in a diagonal, from top right to bottom left. A culture which sustains the corner of complex organization (top right) facilitates coordination with a suitably complex ordering of space and time. The freest is the isolate who is not trying to coordinate anything; the most aggressive is the egalitarian enclavist whose attempts to achieve complex coordination are frustrated by principles that forbid making distinctions between persons.

CULTURE IN AN ADVERSARIAL DEMOCRACY

In the late 1970s Michael Thompson began to collaborate closely with Aaron Wildavsky, and together they introduced several theoretical developments into cultural theory (Ellis, Thompson, and Wildavsky 1990). Starting from the initial assumption that each cultural type is built on a distinctive worldview, Thompson sharpened and refined the idea of opposition between worldviews by introducing the terms "contradictory certainties" and "plural rationalities." A culture builds legitimacy on its own foundation of certainties that contradict the certainties of each of the other cultures. Thus cultures are self-defined adversarially. This second idea, that they need the adversary in order to know who they are and what they stand for, introduces dynamism into the model. The theory now assumes that in any community all four kinds of culture are potentially present, usually actualized, and in continual conflict. Ideally, no one culture would be suppressed by the others. Inevitably, the culture of the isolates is crowded out of the forum, because by definition it is not organized. The adversary relationship of the other three is the essence of democracy. Whether they are referring to immigration, to the municipal rubbish dump, or to the new road, the members of the town meeting are arguing about cultural bias. The contest is about which opposed set of normative values and its attendant social forms will prevail.

With his cartoon of the pioneer, the holyman, and the bureaucrat (Figure 4), Christian Brunner (1989) has drawn three of our

Figure 4. Swiss commentary on cultural theory: the pioneer; the holy-man; the bureaucrat. *Source:* Brunner 1989: 8–9.

missing persons, the politically active persons of cultural theory. The individualist is dressed up as the pioneer; in his working clothes, pickax at hand, he is smugly self-sufficient. The sectarian, enclavist, holyman has a halo and wings and a pure white robe. The hierarchist is the bureaucrat carrying his briefcase; he looks arrogant. The three are not in the postures of debate, but we can see already how they are going to respond to each other.

By reducing the number of viable ways of living in society to a list of four, cultural theory affords a flexible way of thinking about the inherently social human person. Instead of one person, it presents four competing dominant microcosms. Three of the cultures are always in active confrontation. In chapter 6 we shall show them as perennial sources of public-policy proposals.

Correspondingly, the model of the person now incorporates three- or four-sided cultural conflict. By adapting Dennett's culture-free model we can go beyond the homogenized representative individual of current social theory. The persons at each level are interpreting the behavior of other persons as clues to the cultural environment, but they are only seeing the alien behavior through their own cultural lenses. What does the outside of a hierarchy look like to an egalitarian? And vice versa, how can a hierarchist understand what is going on in an egalitarian sect?

EGO MULTIPLIED BY FOUR

Now we are ready to offer an articulated concept of the person. For ego's makeup all we need is the diagram, Figure 3, relabeled to show the opposing cultural tendencies held in internal tension. The four extremes fighting inside ego's psyche are ranked according to ego's place in the organization. Does ego occupy a central position or a peripheral one? If ego is on the periphery, is it as an isolate or involved in a dissenting group? Or if ego is influential, is it as an entrepreneurial individualist or as a bureaucrat? Which organization counts most depends on the kind of question we are trying to answer.

Once we have sketched ego's social environment we can trace on the same little diagram the psyche's conflicting tendencies and desires as they push this way and that. Thus we start to have a unified social theory of the person that is compatible with the demands of the dominant culture, that also incorporates politics, and remains objective. Some cultural theorists would leave the theory there. But perhaps more should be said now about what it implies for psychology. If personality attributes are randomly distributed through a population, it is plausible that certain personalities will be attracted to one rather than to another of the possible cultures and will make life choices accordingly. In any case, we should expect early training to have the same effect. Persons trained in hierarchical assumptions would tend to seek their most congenial and familiar social environment. This would produce in each quadrant a majority of personality types that do well in its cultural climate. It explains how people cluster and how they behave, but it carefully avoids treating personality as an independent variable.

Each of the three articulated worlds—the world of the isolate is inarticulate—is in itself a way of typifying and selecting. The articulation brings finesse to the program of the phenomenologists who are interested in typification. It also protects the researcher from objectivizing criticism, for the simple response is to declare frankly the values from which the premises have been drawn. It is not necessarily a matter of personal preference. There is the vital question of how appropriate a given world is to a given situation.

This is a disciplined form of reflexivity. By studying where you stand in a scheme of possible worlds, you can discover your adversaries and turn the questions about objectivity and consistency back onto them. If the adversary wants an orderly world and at the same time a world of new opportunity, contradiction may ensue; the same applies if the adversary wants an egalitarian world and at the same time expects to dominate it. Research should be designed on a comparative basis, to give due space to the other worlds and their competing values.

The theory puts pressure on the researcher to accord legitimacy to all the cultures. But when this is done, there is still the practical problem. In case of conflict, finding common ground agreeable to all the combatants would entail accepting different accounts of personality types, different interpretation of motives, and different criteria of merit and blame. It would be disingenuous to suggest that the combatants could agree on a just world, for fairness is perceived differently in each culture.

In each of the four cultures acceptable theories of the self would indicate the right kind of education to develop the potential of a child. Speculating, we would be tempted at first to think the education would be more restrictive on the right side of the diagram than on the left, to prepare the child for the exactions of the community on its adult members. But then, we also know that the competitive individualist regime puts severe pressures on the child to prepare for a life of unremitting competition. Because they are communitarian, both cultures on the right side of the diagram would emphasize moral education. Standard ideas about punishment would also reflect the cultural regime and ideas about deviants, conformity, politeness, aggression, and so on. There does not need to be any context-independent theorizing in psychology. The main work ahead is to examine the openness of the individual to the cultural environment.

Figure 5 depicts the four individuals respectively committed to a quadrant of the diagram on Figure 3 above. This indicates how the individual is formed by interacting with the judgments of others. In the individualist quadrant the person is expected to be robust; in the egalitarian quadrant, fragile; in the isolate's quadrant, mysteriously unpredictable; and in the hierarchical one, in need of structure. In each case we would expect the theories of education and developmental psychology to vary in the appropriate directions.

Person Unpredictable

Person Needs Structure

Person Robust

Person Under Duress

Figure 5. Four selves in four cultures: **A** = person robust; **B** = person unpredictable; **C** = person needs structure; **D** = person under duress. (Drawing by Pat Novy)

THE CULTURE OF HOUSEHOLDS

The family is probably the best site for understanding the tremendous tensions triggered by the effort to organize. People are free to run their homes in all sorts of ways. No one tells them to have meals punctually or to have meals at all. They do not need to make their beds, to keep the living room tidy, or to wash up; and coordination does not come automatically. Yet if they do adopt a time pattern, or if they refuse to adopt one at all, the choice rules out other things they might do, and tension will

ensue. Going from the family up to higher levels of organization, any members of the community may find it oppressive to
submit to careful ordering, and it follows that at all times a complex organization can provoke breakaway tendencies in its ranks.

Social science survey research has put the family through the
same homogenizing process as the individual. If families are not
all the same, it is thought enough to look for demographic differences, number and age of dependents, parents' occupation,
and so on. The idea that families might be run on different principles is well known in family sociology, but as yet little attention
has been given to different household cultures. There is no theoretical niche into which to fit the information that some households do not centralize the family budget, that timetables might
or might not be rigorously kept, or that chores might be distributed systematically or left to free negotiation. The theory of culture is such a theoretical niche, and illuminating household studies have distinguished all four types of household cultures simply
by concentrating on uses of time and space and on control of
resources. If people are organizing differently, they are thinking
differently about organization and also about morals, society, and
identity.

Karl Dake and Michael Thompson developed instruments of
inquiry for assessing household structuration—that is, regulation—and incorporation—that is, group boundaries—with two
sets of inquiries, one based on anthropological interviews and
another based on quantitative methods. Figure 6 sums up some
of their results.

Dake and Thompson examined how patterns of social relationships affect household management. The hierarchists have
regular routines, cherish family traditions, save up for holidays,

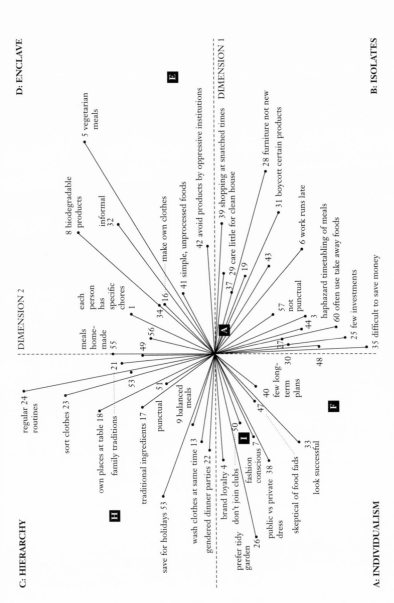

Figure 6. Household cultures and self-reported behavior. *Source:* Dake 1993: 431.

and, among other things, have punctual meals. The households labeled here as isolates do none of these things: They do not value punctuality, find saving difficult, have haphazard time-tabling of meals, and resort to take-out foods. The diagram emphasizes the cultural contrast between the right and left side of the diagram in Figure 3.

RECLASSIFYING THE NINE CITIES OF NEWPORT AND THE FIVE FRENCH WORLDS

Looking again at Wilder's nine cities in Newport, we can ignore the two archeological ones, because they are uninhabited; and we can ignore, because they are isolated worlds in themselves, the seaport, the military and naval bases, and the handful of intellectuals. That leaves four contemporary cities interacting with each other. Wealth and class are not good criteria for classifying according to culture, so we put the traditionalist burghers of the ninth city in with the servants of the seventh city. The vulgar summer visitors of the sixth city uphold an individualist philosophy of life, tending to make their own rules ad hoc, so we place them on the map diagonally opposite their own tradition-minded servants and the merchants. Wilder has classed the would-be intruders of the eighth city separately from the would-be excluders, but the anthropological scheme would class the fortune seekers and adventurers with the rich visitors: They are also individualists, with the same attitudes toward money and people.

It is not difficult to spread the fictional Newport over the diagram, but the four contemporary cities only fill two culturally distinct slots. Newport has no evangelical churches or egalitarian communes, no one speaking in tongues, no charismatics, no groups of demonstrators breaking windows. As a model of cultural bias Wilder's scheme is incomplete, because although he has hier-archists, individualists, and isolates, he has left out one of the usual components of civil society: There should be a city in Newport, or several, organized for collective protest against the manners and morals of the others.

The justificatory universe of the French sociologists has to bear a similar reproach. There are six different scenarios, but only two distinct cultural biases: the world of opinion, the world of industry, and the world of commerce are only socioeconomic variants of the same culture. They share competitive values, manifested in different ways. Similarly, the world of legal statutes and the domestic world are organized on hierarchical principles, like the City of God, manifest at different levels of organization. If they wanted to show all the main varieties of justification, the sociologists should also have included a sectarian type, as well as isolates who tend to justify everything by good or bad luck. It just goes to show how the imagination needs to be prodded and how a method helps to find the gaps.

ISOLATES

Wilder's Newport actually does have some isolates to fill the top left-hand corner of the diagram. They are wives and daughters in the sixth city, frustrated, neglected, hemmed in by restrictive rules. The young hero finds these ladies in chains and liberates them. The principles of differentiation he has used to distinguish the other cities do not allow him to count these women as a city, because they are not spatially, chronologically, or occupationally segregated, but they are isolated nonetheless and share some cultural bias even if they do not know each other.

Twentieth-century social sciences have been working steadily on the distinction between communitarian hierarchy and individualist market. The contrast between the two extremes of the diagonal that links hierarchy with individualism is familiar to us and presents no problem. It is easy to see that markets and hierarchies embrace different values and a different idea of the good.

It is more difficult to incorporate in the normal political science conversation the other two cultures, isolates and egalitarian groups. The first tend to be ignored because they are voiceless; the second, though often strident, tend to be ignored because they are relegated to the chapter on religion. The isolates are very interesting in themselves, a category of people who have somehow dropped out from the constitutional debates going on around them, perhaps unintentionally or perhaps because they were forced out by the fierceness of the competition or were destined to the margins by some personal inadequacy or congenital defect. Because by definition they collaborate with each other minimally, it may seem contrived to speak of them as having a cultural bias. But the very fact of somehow not being caught up in other people's time schedules, not trying to exert influence, and not seeking power gives them something in common. The isolate's style is lightheartedness, even fecklessness, or alternatively, putting a brave face on hopelessness, on fatalism. Having no way to direct outcomes, it is easier not to reflect deeply on the policy choices of the day and to embrace a genial fatalism (Douglas 1996). A great deal of a community's fate depends on what proportion of its citizens have slipped into this cultural condition and are unresponsive to exhortation and warnings alike.

Take, for example, the issue of plural democracy. By definition, the isolate is marginalized and excluded from the political arena. This could be a dilemma for cultural theorists who also believe in the normative value of plural democracies. If we hold on to the assumptions of cultural theory—namely, that there will always be isolates and that isolation is a "viable way of life" (Ellis, Thompson, and Wildavsky 1990)—then plural democracies can never fully live up to their democratic aspirations of involving all the citizens in the policy process.

It has been sociologists' contention that the evolutionary tendencies of advanced capitalist societies have resulted in more and more people being forced into social isolation. As traditional forms of social integration have been swept away by the tidal waves of two technological revolutions—industrial and informational—gaping holes have been left in the social fabric. The right way to relate to one another is in dialogue.

Jürgen Habermas (1962, 1973, 1987b) has a general thesis that the modern public sphere has deteriorated and lost the political function of legitimizing policy. As the public sphere and the state become increasingly interdependent, citizens are withdrawing to the intimate sphere of their nuclear families. Public debate of policy issues has become a technical discussion by experts who come up with policy recommendations that are then sold to a depoliticized public. As the citizens' input into policy decisions is increasingly reduced, a tendency that Habermas calls civic privatism (*Staatsbürgelicher Privatismus*) becomes evident. And as citizens become more interested in the administrative and compensatory services available—child support, unemployment

benefits, and the like—they increasingly lose interest in partici-
pating in the legitimization process (Habermas 1973: 106).
According to Habermas, isolation goes hand in hand with loss of
civic input, which in turn is a result of advanced capitalism.

The Rowntree Inquiry into Income and Wealth (1995), a
social survey of income distribution in Britain, has recently con-
firmed these theoretical considerations. Among other things, the
report pointed to an increasing percentage of the population that
was being permanently excluded from the economic system and
forced into isolation. The report found that crime, drug abuse,
and political extremism can be retraced to "groups of disaffected
young men with no role in and no stake in society or in an economy for which they have no skills which are valued. The economic forces which have left this group marginalized seem likely
to us to continue and to intensify; unless something is done to
reintegrate these groups, all of society will end up suffering the
consequences" (Rowntree Foundation 1995: 34).

As we will see in chapter 6, a cultural analysis of the policy
process, replete with the theoretically inelegant isolate, allows us
to think about pluralist democracies in terms of who is being
excluded from public debate and social interaction. A system that
forces many into social, economic, and political isolation is failing in the stated ideals of pluralist democracy. Thus, we have to
view the four cultures in their normal adversarial mode, each
poised against the others and each struggling to overcome the
organizational disadvantages that follow from their respective
cultural posture.

CHAPTER SIX

Persons in the Policy Process

In our grandparents' day two topics were banned in polite company: religion and politics. The taboo made for dull conversation, but the amenities were preserved and no one dashed his or her drink in another guest's face or even stormed out of the party. Does it matter whether analysts theorize blandly about a pale *Homo œconomicus* without blood or bile? Bland urbanity may be a good way to discuss important issues, but it should not trivialize public policy by sidestepping major issues or by adopting a partisan view. It is not necessary to call a spade a spade, but it is necessary to know what a spade is.

ATROCITIES, OUTRAGE, AND RECIPROCAL INSULTS

Policymakers from hierarchies attend peace conferences where they meet their enclavist opposite numbers. The professional diplomats are men and women of the world. They discount the bizarre costume of the enclavist spokespersons; they expect them to meet their own conciliatory move with intransigence; they know they have to seem unyielding if their people are watching or the press is in attendance; they are used to stalemates. They know how to deal urbanely with everything else, but they cannot deal with the insults against their own ideas of justice. In this they are no better protected from anger and righteousness than are the enclavists. Without knowing how the parties are organized and how their organization affects their behavior, the frustration of the peace conference drives the hierarchists to resort to the usual iron fist and the enclavists to the usual riots. The real problems go far deeper than the textbooks can say.

It is not true that the enclavist sectarians are the only intransigent culture. Hierarchists and individualists can be equally ruthless and destructive, but they have a more extensive sociological archive. The enclavists have mainly been studied under the rubric of religion, so they are known to us as they appear to the idealist gaze of the humanities. We know a great deal about their religious views, always presented as eccentricities in the field of ideas, and about their leaders' personalities, always presented as the explanations of what happens. But we know next to nothing about their organizational problems. This gap we will try to remedy in this and the following chapters.

The enclave culture is inherently factional and prone to splitting. William McNeil is right to see its tremendous powers for renewal. He hopes that "contemporary fundamentalist movements will be the seedbeds of future religious communities that might stabilize world-wide urban society" (McNeil 1993: 573). However, we may cast doubt on his optimism. He underrates the disruptive power of divergent ideas of justice which are inherent in different ways of life.

Writing as an anthropologist, Paul Richards (1996b) describes a devastating civil war going on then in West Africa as a "dramaturgy of violence." In Sierra Leone the violence by one side against the other is as deliberately outrageous as anything the English have suffered from the IRA or that the Lebanese and Israelis inflict on each other. The anger is even more inflamed. The rebel movement in Sierra Leone, Richards argues, has embarked on violence, seeking to redress some of the most urgent contradictions of a "global" and ecologically damaging underdevelopment. The antidote to the cultural inventiveness of rebel terror and violence, he continues, will come not from ignoring or rubbishing their efforts but through supporting those who understand the nature of the gap that has to be bridged and who command the local cultural resources to do something about it.

To understand what is happening Richards has to dredge through the past tragic history of injustice and betrayal. The forest egalitarians could see their world being changed, perhaps destroyed, by the rampant acquisitiveness of hunters, traders, slavers, loggers—and, more recently, diamond dealers. They knew that their chiefs, in order to survive in a changing world, had entered into off-the-record deals with these agents of international "primitive accumulation" (Richards 1996a). In Richards's view, a long-term and total failure of justice has lit the flames of passion in Sierra Leone. At the institutional level, it is a story of power abused and accountability hopelessly lost; on the personal side, a story of disillusionment and despair. Both sides accuse each other of atrocities, often with perfect truth. The young rebel forces and their supporters accuse their enemy of cannibalism, the most atrocious crime imaginable. Clearly there cannot be peace until the intense mutual repugnance is overcome, the horror of the victims' desecrated bodies made to fade, and the fury of the aggressors appeased. For the theory of public policy not to reach this level of discord is to be irrelevant. One reason it cannot go deeper is that the validity of other cultures is denied. The policy analysts claim to speak objectively but always stay close to their own cultural vantage point.

BOUNDED RATIONALITY

Utility theory presupposes a human brain that is capable of impossibly elaborate calculations. Herbert Simon, seeing this flaw, suggested that instead of aiming to maximize satisfaction, as supposed by the theory, rationality is bounded as to its scope and power, and the rational being aims not to maximize but to satisfice, that is, to find a zone of satisfaction with several criteria (Simon 1947). In this approach, bounded rationality is not necessarily negative, although many commentators have seen boundedness as a limitation on rational thought (Williamson 1975). The argument we have been developing about the minds of social beings suggests, on the contrary, that bounded rationality is a special kind of human cleverness that allows the individual mind to hand over some of the work of thinking to habit or to institutions. It is not just an economy in psychic energy or just a skill for avoiding overload but a way of tapping into the experience of other persons. Is this a weakness? Your answer depends on what sort of bias you have about institutions or, to put it into the same terms, how you regard this faculty depends on the way your reasoning is bounded. It is only following a particular cultural bias to assume, as public-policy teaching does, that decision making occurs in a social vacuum. An alternative view is that the faculty of rational bounding is open to cultural influences—in which case policy studies should take into account cultural bias.

In the established view, public policy is the result of the interplay of different groups in the political system: Interest groups and pressure groups jostle for influence and position with the state. Each of these groups is described in terms of the rational-choice microcosm: They are removed from their social contexts and aggregated, so policymaking becomes the interaction of hypothetical individuals.

The normative basis for conventional policy sciences is pluralist theory, as advocated by Robert Dahl (1961) or Nelson Polsby (1980). Pluralism's central message is that power in advanced capitalist societies is sufficiently diffused to allow everyone reasonable access to decision making. The message provides both the ethical and methodological backbones of the policy sciences: Good government is pluralist government, and the policy scientists test the quality of government from an individualist perspective. Policy analysis should restrict itself to individual decisions that emanate from discrete individual units. They suppose that policy problems materialize from individual choices, policy actors respond with solution strategies, and then decisions are made—case closed.

However, some policy analysts, drawing on work that is broadly described as social constructivist (Becker 1963; Berger and Luckmann 1966; MacLeod and Saraga 1988), argue that the individualist conception of well-being inherited from liberalism wrongly restricts the pluralist scope of inquiry to formal issues and decisions about them. They consider the idea that we can study issues and decisions while disregarding the social processes from which they emerge as a typical liberal reification.

Ideology should not rule the day, for the democratic claims of advanced capitalist society are supposed to be objective; and if it is true that all policymaking has an ideological dimension, the pluralist's claim to universality is imperiled.

CULTURAL BIAS IN THE POLICY PROCESS

In chapter 5 we identified four cultures, each established on fundamentally opposed principles. Each rests on a distinctive form of organization, with its own "justifying ideas which tend to be invoked as if part of the natural order" (Douglas and Wildavsky 1983: 6). Each has a distinctive definition of well-being that it would like public policy to achieve.

Individualists, as the name implies, are not trying to create a community but rather aiming to free themselves from the fetters of social restriction. They thrive in loose organizational structures, around which they can move freely without long-term commitment, able to negotiate their own dealings with other individuals. Well-being for them means the freedom to pursue self-interested ends. It is the well-being of the narrowly defined ego, the ideal of negative freedom from interference. The strong policy angle is that individualists would consider that rational persons, though not equal, are best situated to judge what is good for themselves.

Hierarchists seek to make a community that is an orderly system; their moral framework is one of differentiated obligations according to place in complex organizational schemes. Hierarchists have a broader, longer-term, stratified conception of well-being. The happiness of others enters into individual well-being. According to status and position in the hierarchy, well-being may be different for lower-echelon members than for the elite. Hierarchists do not consider it impossible to judge others' needs, and it may be properly legitimate for high-status members of the hierarchy to decide and act in the best interest of their charges. This is a major difference in policy style from the above.

Sectarian minority groups strive to create a community that is free of control. Morally, they appeal to subjectivity and individual conscience. At the level of organization they frown on formal discriminations and are the champions of communal self-organization. Sectarians perceive well-being on a global scale: Everyone is equal, and well-being is a world free of domination and inequality. This principle is not open to negotiation; there is no middle ground. On policy issues this is a style of thinking and a substantive policy package that is totally different from the two above.

Isolates are by definition cut off from political maneuvering and influence. They do not have a coherent idea of well-being and do not expect coherence from policymakers. If you are lucky, you will do well; if not, then not.

The cultures all maintain their vitality by enacting their mutual symbolic opposition. All contact with others is in terms of the culture's own assumptions and social relationships (Luhmann 1984; for a biological model of self-generation, see Maturana and Varela 1980). The ideas they entertain about the motivations of others are produced in their everyday normative talk and reflect back to them what cultural opposition leads them to expect. For example, in the global climate change (GCC) debate the sectarian Greens comment on the work of economists only in terms of exploited power differentials and inequalities. Aubrey Meyer's view of proposals by economists to evaluate the environment using cost-benefit analysis is that economists "seek only to promote the whirlwind romance of partnership for profits" and that their policy proposals will be "neither equitable nor sustainable, in reality or intent" (Meyer 1994: 2–3).

Thus, by interpreting the intentions of stereotypical others according to the language of cultural conflict, each culture achieves logical closure on its premises and succeeds in reproducing its own system of control and accountability. Cultures incorporate their implicit agendas by framing selected issues, setting agendas, labeling, and foregrounding, backgrounding, and fading out. In policy analysis, pluralist theory itself, with all its commitment to objectivity, is a process of foregrounding. This reasonable requirement that criticism should be backed by evidence is deployed as a kind of epistemological skepticism in favor of objectivity and against subjective arguments. Combined with adherence to the rational choice paradigm, it produces a framing device for the worthwhile questions. At the same time, of course, it excludes certain other questions that come from other cultural viewpoints and need specially collected evidence. Take, for example, the question of whose voices are heard in the policy process.

A pluralist political system is supposed to be one in which power is widely dispersed among the different social groups. No one group becomes dominant or tyrannous, and everyone has the possibility of having his or her voice heard. The excluded question is: What counts as a voice? or What counts as a group? Usually a group is taken to be a collection of individuals who have come together with an opinion. It is expected that different minorities, ethnic and religious, local and cosmopolitan, will have voices in the political debate.

Yet in any community at least three and possibly four cultural voices with four political agendas are speaking and ought to be heard. Genuine political pluralism would have to be extended so that no one of the four cultural voices dominates the policy process and pursues its agenda for collective well-being to the exclusion of the others. Access to policymaking would have to be assured to the individualists, the hierarchists, the sectarians, and the isolates. Democratic freedom would mean that no one of the cultures would be excluded from the debate or marginalized from the action. This is very different from trying to ensure that the voice of every linguistic or ethnic group is heard. As a tactic it offers hope of smoothing the path of politics before the unforgivable injustices can take place and before the hostilities harden.

THE CULTURAL-ARGUMENT SYSTEM

In chapter 7 we will show that relationships between cultures are inherently conflictual. How, then, will they ever agree to share power? Do they even want to? We hear a sectarian voice declaring that it cannot compromise. Sharing a political conversation may be easier. Perhaps cultural diversity may be accommodated by the so-called argumentative turn in public-policy analysis.

Certain policy analysts focus on the argumentative process. For them, policymaking entails "the actual performances of argumentation and the practical rhetorical work of framing analyses, articulating them, [and] constructing senses of value and significance" (Fischer and Forester 1993: 5). The public sphere is not a place where public opinion miraculously crystallizes from a collection of atomized, individual opinions. Policy arguments must reflect the social contexts from which they emerge; the conflicting norms and aspirations provide the basis for policy conflict. In the public sphere these policy arguments are produced and pitted against each other.

Among many approaches, Maarten Hajer's idea of a discourse coalition captures this notion best. For him, a discourse coalition is "a group of actors who share a social construct" (Hajer 1993: 43). Social constructs give a clear meaning to ambiguous social circumstances; they are means of ordering events. Social constructs are informed by discourse, through which they "can be tied to specific institutions and actors" (pp. 43–46). Discourse coalitions battle in the public sphere for legitimacy. They construct policy arguments and try to incorporate them in policy. We can think of them as cultures in dialogue. Hajer illustrates his thesis with the struggle in the 1980s of two discourse coalitions, traditional pragmatism and ecomodernism, in the British acid-rain debate.

The former, traditional pragmatism, had grown out of the regulatory apparatus of British environmental policy dating from the nineteenth century. Arguing from a typically hierarchical position, the traditional pragmatists favored science-based, human-health-biased, and industry-friendly solutions to environmental problems which would obviate the need for confrontation. The ecomodernists, on the other hand, were typically speaking in a sectarian voice. They represented more contemporary ideas about the politics of the environment. Not afraid of conflict, they sought to impose tough minimum standards and hefty fines and did not shy from confrontation with industry: For them, the environment had intrinsic value. Each side disputed the other's scientific evidence, and both attempted to persuade other policy actors of the value of their respective approaches.

Hajer did not specify a third discourse coalition, but it is not difficult to find examples from other policy disputes. Brendan Swedlow (1994) identifies three arguments concerning mental-health policy, corresponding to the three politically active cultures. According to the "thank-you theory of paternalistic intervention" (Swedlow 1994: 73), medical professionals and experts can and should make decisions on behalf of the mentally ill if they are not fit to decide for themselves—which is, of course, a judgment that falls to the expert. Mandatory incarceration and institutionalization of the mentally ill—that is, subjecting the patients to professional control—may often be the only road to good mental health. For Swedlow this approach expresses the hierarchical bias in mental-health administration: Expert psychiatrists (high status), the argument goes, are in a more suitable position to define not only their patients' well-being but also the most appropriate means of attaining it.

In contrast, the sectarian "preoccupation with power differentials and inequities" (Swedlow 1994: 78) would lead to the construction of a different policy argument. Mental illness, the sectarians would typically argue, is caused by oppressive inequality in the social environment. Consequently, the right treatment must be to provide egalitarian conditions for patients. Swedlow cites institutions such as Kingsley Hall, in London, where the boundaries between patients and staff are deliberately blurred for therapeutic purposes (p. 78). True to the sectarian orientation, well-being of the mentally ill is incorporated in the well-being of humanity as a whole: Mental illness is merely a symptom of a deeper social malaise of prevailing inequality.

Finally, Swedlow identifies a libertarian approach associated with Thomas Szasz that places great emphasis on autonomy, freedom, and personal development. Here, mental illness is just one of many equally legitimate human conditions. Strongly opposed to the institutionalization of the mentally ill, the libertarians favor contractual arrangements between individual patient and doctor (Swedlow 1994: 80). Psychiatrists have no special abilities that would justify determining what is good for the patient. Szasz's epistemological skepticism is characteristic of the individualist culture and in profound contradiction with the hierarchists' confidence in what they know.

These examples illustrate how distinctive cultures produce policy arguments that, at least implicitly, articulate the culture's construction of well-being and vie for legitimacy in the public sphere. If one of those cultures starts to dominate public policy in a certain professional field, we have a good clue as to how the professionals stand as a group in relation to the rest of the society.

THINKING ABOUT CONFLICT
IN THE PUBLIC SPHERE

In pluralist theory a comforting analogy holds between the political sphere and the marketplace. Decisions in the public sphere are reached in an incremental and disjointed fashion (Lindblom 1965). Policymakers muddle through, and policy decisions are eventually coordinated through the benign guidance of the invisible hand. Like the free market, the policy process is self-organizing, and political groups are supposed to gravitate toward a natural equilibrium.

David Collingridge argues attractively that "efficient trial and error learning cannot be a solitary affair; it is essentially social" (1992: 7), a claim we would wholly endorse. Alas! when he goes on to illustrate what he means by a social process it turns out to be no more than interaction between rational individuals: "Markets, of course, are a wonderful example of efficient learning about demand and supply of goods and services: here forecasts can be revised very quickly and at no real cost" (p. 7). According to Collingridge, this learning machinery which tends to compromise is evident in all areas of life. In the case of a conflict of opinion, the parties will, rather than delaying for years, "agree to a rough and ready compromise which can be implemented quickly" (p. 8). Coordination of policy decisions "is accomplished by the mutual adjustment of many people" (p. 8), which obviates the need for central coordination—and this is where he leaves it.

Collingridge acknowledges the social character of consensus in the public sphere, yet he reverts back to the individualist market model, which strips the individual of social attributes. He attributes to market adjustments an unconscious quality: Competing views enter the market, and consensus appears as if by magic. This may work if the individual is reduced to minimal attributes; that is, if he or she has no social ties or ethical commitments. Then all rational individuals will discount policy arguments in the same manner. Hence policy-coordination problems are solved automatically, and policy conflict does not have to be written into the political system.

This is grossly inaccurate. Policy conflicts can show a degree of absolute intransigence that no market mechanism can solve. For example, the French decision in 1995 to resume nuclear testing in the South Pacific sparked a conflict between France and Southern Hemisphere governments that no amount of incremental adjustment would have solved. Similarly, the battle between environmental groups and the Royal Dutch / Shell group of companies concerning the sinking of the decommissioned oil rig, the *Brent Spar*, was resolved only by Shell's backing down after a consumer boycott. In the controversy about commercial whaling, the terms of argument are absolute: Environmentalists call for an unqualified halt to all whaling (Peterson 1992).

If we allow for cultural diversity in the public sphere, we must acknowledge that there is bound to be systemic disagreement over fundamental principles. Whole social persons will not be able to resolve disagreement as easily as will the abstract unsocial persons of the market model. Policy options acceptable to some will almost certainly be morally repugnant to others. The individual market model cannot account for irreconcilable disagreement. And if this impasse is reached, one thing that will not help is to preach virtue to the opposing parties.

CIVIC RESPONSIVENESS

Robert Putnam (1993) has traced the difference in performance of Italian regional governments to what he calls "civic virtues." These civic virtues are norms of reciprocity, trust, solidarity, and tolerance that facilitate the consensus-seeking democratic process. It is as if civic virtues form a stock of moral resources from which citizens can draw in their everyday interaction with others. But everything we have so far presented indicates that civic virtues do not exist except as an integral part of a dynamic policy process in a culturally balanced constitution. It is better to think of the virtues as the norms that regulate interaction than as a Mother Hubbard's larder from which the citizens can help themselves to some civic nourishment whenever they need to resolve a conflict.

Pluralist theory promised a method of ascertaining how well late-capitalist political systems live up to democratic ideals. But the liberal individualist microcosm got in the way. Pluralist theorists have taken their idea of well-being from the individualist program. They may be right when they tell us that the democratic institutions in advanced capitalism effectively safeguard well-being under this definition. But members of other cultures may be faring badly in the realization of their differently defined ideals. Pluralist theorists are unable to take other cultural definitions of well-being into account.

The quality of a political system depends on the quality of communication in the public sphere. An argument can be stonewalled or rationally discussed; it can be made into a key issue or defined out of existence. The question that was ruled out of court—the question of whose voice counts—is the crucial one. In a pluralist public sphere, policy actors have to be responsive to policy arguments from rival cultures. Some policy debates are very vibrant: Everyone chimes in, and a variety of voices is heard. This is a good state of affairs if it means that every cultural bias is represented. In other cases it seems as if one booming voice drowns everything else out. We can use the term "civic responsiveness" to describe the first kind, whereas the second is a monologue unresponsive to dissenting voices.

Putnam charted the changing attitudes of Italian regional politicians. As can be seen in Table 4, Italian politicians in successful regions became more and more open to compromise and open to

TABLE 4.   THE DEPOLARIZATION
OF REGIONAL COUNCILORS IN ITALY (IN PERCENTAGES)

	1970	1976	1981/1982	1989
Extremist	42	31	21	40
Moderate	58	69	79	86
Total	100 (72)	100 (154)	100 (151)	100 (166)

SOURCE: Putnam 1993: 31.

policy proposals from opposing parties. Furthermore, the same time period saw a depolarization of policy, with a steady shift to centrist issues. In effect, Putnam has charted a steady increase in civic responsiveness in northern Italian regions. Although the political groups still remain divided on fundamental issues (such as the role of the Roman Catholic church), opposing policy arguments are taken seriously and debated openly. It should be stressed that this convergence of attitudes occurred irrespective of regional politicians who aspired to fulfill liberal ideals. In fact, the most successful region in terms of civic responsiveness, Emilia Romagna, has been under Communist rule for the past twenty years.

Civic responsiveness could provide a gauge of pluralist politics in a culturally diverse public sphere: Putnam has shown that measures can be devised. Whether citizens can expect prompt replies from authorities when they lodge a complaint can be assessed. Whether the forms for filing benefit or health claims are in the languages spoken in the community can be ascertained. Whether the individuals can receive answers from their Members of Parliament is there on paper; there is nothing subjective about it. Some questions are less capable of exact measurement:

whether policy debate has become an exchange of abuse; whether deviant lifestyles are tolerated or set up as scapegoats; whether the moral views of the citizens are suppressed in favor of the technical views of expert opinion. Yet there is no reason why these aspects of civic responsiveness cannot also be objectively researched and assessed.

Frank Hendriks's study of urban road planning in Birmingham and Munich provides an example. The two cities showed marked differences in their approaches, which Hendriks described as running from "monocultural hegemony [Birmingham] to multicultural pluralism [Munich]" (Hendriks 1994: 51). The pluralistic approach in Munich led to "sustainable and liveable" public policy (p. 51), whereas Birmingham's road system is what could be at best termed chaotic and misanthropic. The traffic flows are the test that show civic responsiveness to be higher in Munich than in Birmingham.

Conversely, norms of civic responsiveness in the international debate about GCC are virtually absent. Agreement can only be reached at the lowest of denominators; namely, that the Earth is at risk from carbon dioxide emissions. From that point the debate shifts from reducing carbon dioxide to the viability of the capitalist system itself: The opposed cultures are entrenched in their extreme positions, and no middle ground can be found. The Greens accuse the economists of greed and ideological obfuscation and the hierarchists of imperial neglect. The individualists dismiss all debate by insisting that the Green vision of the future is naively utopian and that hierarchical schemes of rational management are the source of pollution. The hierarchists accuse the Greens of political radicalism and the individualists of dangerous adventurism. Deadlock is a sign that civic responsiveness is low:

Carbon dioxide emissions continue to increase with very little restraint.

In conclusion, we do not know whether the open, intercultural dialogue will rectify the political hegemony that generates the bitter sense of injustice, but we do believe that the dialogue will tend to monologue if the underlying cultural conflicts are not recognized. We emphatically endorse the old idea that attentive bureaucratic response is the only way to proceed toward plural democracy. There is nothing original or profound in this bland and nondivisive approach. Much more interesting is the question of the extent to which the sense of injustice arises from blatant acts of injustice or from inventiveness called forth by the cultural conflict itself. This is the focus of our discontent with crisis theories and deprivation theories of social unrest. There are pressures that drive political creativity, invention of new outrages, and new forms of equality whose infringement is mortally insulting. Not to know where these energies come from will ultimately be disabling to public policy.

CHAPTER SEVEN

The Adversarial Mode

RISK AS THE FORUM
FOR CULTURAL CONFLICT

An old Chinese curse says: "May you ever live in interesting times!" When we reflect on the life of a community built around antagonistic cultures, each defining itself against the others, keeping the balance emerges as the most difficult task. Interesting times are always around the corner and discord is too much with us, always ready to erupt.

A funnel effect is at work, gathering separate issues to the same focus, pouring the pent-up anger out of one spout. In religious cultures that focusing agent is the idea of God. Too many issues disperse the efforts; too many gods end up being distributed between antagonists. Appealing to the justice of one god is a unifying strategy. It captures some common ground from which the cultural debate can proceed. This centering process results in the microcosm effects we discussed in chapter 2. If the culture is entirely pluralist, determined to respect a diversity of religious beliefs, what sort of central focus can there be? Or if the culture is entirely secular? Can human rights be formulated to fill the role? The difficulties surface as soon as we remember how much cultural life depends on each culture producing its variant definitions of the person, morality, and basic rights.

Risk has become a way of talking about justice when the parties to the debate, not sharing the same history or institutions, have different ways of articulating their ideas of right and wrong. They do not belong to the same church; they cannot appeal to formulated doctrine or directly to God; they need a bridging concept. Current international and national political debates have narrowed many separate issues to the single one of risk, whether it is risk to persons, or to the environment, or to the economy.

Risk is actually a complex idea, but it has become through these usages a simple rhetorical strategy for forcing difficult issues into the open. In French academic circles risk has already started to provide a new vocabulary for questions of justice and justification (Duclos 1991; Laufer 1993). In Germany Ulrich Beck has made the first stab at rewriting all of political science in terms of vulnerability to risk (Beck 1992). But no one has sorted out the issue of who perceives the risks. Without going beyond the single representative rational individual and developing a theory of cultural types, common sense becomes enmeshed in the spectacular contradictions of the risk debates. One benefit of cultural theory is to allow space for standing back from the fight.

A risk perception is a perception of danger, and it cannot make sense to isolate it from the perceiver's life project or from the other ideas the person has of good and bad and the way to live. As we know by now, cultural theory approaches all political issues with a model of four kinds of rational being, each representing one of four kinds of cultural bias. Any case of risk perception would be linked to one of four kinds of other perceptions, based on four rival political and moral agendas.

Risk perception brought under the lens of cultural theory illustrates the minimalist idea of the social being modeled in the preceding chapter. The social person will use everything—including risks—to engage with or disengage from or somehow control other persons. This view gives full value to the adversarial nature of risk as an accusation. The political context has to be drawn in, and the moral aspects of the issues at stake must be sought.

In a hierarchical culture a new risk is filed along with like cases. It is calmly discussed as a challenge which must, and can, be managed, and there is no reason for panic. The problem is one of classification: Moral aspects are played down and politics excluded; regulation will resolve the problem. In an enclave culture risk is a scenario rife with anger and righteousness. An identified risk has its prospective victims, the suppliers of risk are evil-doers, the accusers are on the side of the angels, and risk is highly politicized. A new risk is like a new weapon in the hands of the embattled enclavists. The individualist entrepreneurs will want to minimize the news of risk, for if it is exaggerated their free action will come under regulation, and they do not want that. When the isolates eventually hear of the danger they will probably shrug it off. They are too fatalist to believe in it, or if they do see the risks, they are too fatalist to believe that anything can or will be done.

In the risk forum the hierarchy—that can be held accountable—and the enclave—that is, the voice of conscience—are cast as diametrically opposed. Whether the risk is to the water supplies, or to food through pesticides, or to human life by infection with mad-cow disease, the former culture will try to minimize the danger and the latter to amplify it. To the ears of the enclavists, nothing that the industrialists—accused of causing it—or the government—accused of permitting it—can say will mitigate the risk because the enclavists do not accept the industrialists' or the government's assumptions. The accused call in technical experts and consult the statistics of harm. The dispute about justice and the proper way to live is deflected to an altercation about percentages, 0.01 per million. The contestants are talking past each other. Does it matter? As long as we know the platform they are speaking from, no, it probably does not. But if we think the oratorical displays are about risks, we are missing the point of the contests.

CULTURAL AUDIT FOR RISK AVERSION

Following on this line of inquiry, Ellis, Thompson, and Wildavsky (1990), proposed that policy analysis ought to have a regular cultural audit to monitor shifts of bias. For example, if the effect of economic depression is to increase the proportion of radical lobbyists in the population, then the diagram would be weighed down on one side, and you would expect a more risk-averse policy to be popular. On the other hand, the cultural effect of economic depression is more devious, so it would have to be researched. Depression could make more people lose their jobs and friends and could thus send them into the top left quadrant of the isolates. In that case in the long run a more happy-go-lucky, unconcerned bias might be expected to prevail: "Leave me alone and let the environment look after itself." With prosperity more of the population could see prospects of independence, the entrepreneurial quadrant would be better represented, and then again, no doubt, the environment would have to take care of itself and strong arguments would be made for deregulation.

The first breakthrough for this kind of analysis was the reanalysis by Karl Dake and Aaron Wildavsky of already gathered survey data on risk perceptions (Dake 1991). Citizens of the San Francisco Bay Area had been questioned about their attitudes toward technology, with the underlying assumption that attitudes to risk would depend on personality traits. The predictions were that egalitarians would

> believe that an inegalitarian society is likely to insult the fragile environment just as it exploits the poor. The predictions for the hierarchist and individualist world views are just the opposite: both are viewed as technologically optimistic—the hierarchists because they believe that the hazards of technology can be managed by their experts in a way that improves the quality of life, and individualists because they see technology as a vehicle for unlimited individual enterprise. Thus it is also hypothesized that hierarchists and individualists will show far less concern than egalitarians about environmental and technological dangers. (Dake 1991: 66)

In the result, egalitarianism turned out to be correlated positively with all the thirty-six so-called societal concerns listed, except one: "loss of respect for authority." The egalitarians are much more worried about social conditions than are the other cultures. This supported the contention that egalitarians as a category are more critical of society, less concerned about upholding its present institutions, and more risk averse than other cultures. Hierarchists and individualists, the left side of our diagram (Figure 3), showed much less concern about technological and environmental dangers. "Threat of nuclear war" ranked near the bottom of the correlates for hierarchy and individualism, and "dangers associated with technology" and "environmental pollution" correlated—to varying degrees—negatively. Hierarchists and individualists were much more concerned about "demonstrations and protests," "civil disobedience," and loss of authority and were less worried about "loss of civil liberties."[1]

The topic of risk is a litmus test for cultural bias. The more a nation moves up the grid toward hierarchy and a strong command system, the less will dangers, even obvious dangers, be noticed. We saw on the television news the aftermath of the Chernobyl nuclear meltdown: The security guards were told to remove the radioactive debris, they were assured there was no danger in picking it up with their bare hands, they went ahead and did it, and they died. In a culture dominated by individualism or enclavism, such unquestioning obedience would be unlikely.

The more a nation moves down the grid toward the culture of the egalitarian enclave, the more the risk debates will be acrimonious and interminable. The people will seem to be craven

---

1. Since then, other questionnaires have been developed to capture variations in public allegiance to the different cultures. It has turned out to be quite difficult to replicate these results outside California, for evidently everything depends on how well the investigators know the local language and political history. No one can pick up these questions and have them make sense in Middle Europe, say, or India, or Japan. Claire Marris, of the University of East Anglia in England, led a team that sought to integrate cultural theory with psychological theory of risk (Marris, Langford, and O'Riordan 1996). Gunnar Grendstad, Per Selle, and Kristin Strömnes (1996), of the University of Bergen in Norway, have worked on political allegiance and environmental policy. Helene Karmasin, director of the survey unit at the Institut für Motivforschung in Vienna, having worked out her own questions to suit the Austrian experience, has been able to find how specially drawn samples polarize on topical issues.

hearted, jumping with terror at every alarm. They say they are afraid of this or that, afraid for themselves or their children, and they demand government regulation to the strangle point. Remember what we said about using fear and other emotions as explanations. The risk debates are political debates: When fear is invoked by one side, understand that the people are not timorous; in fact, quite the contrary, they are being pugnacious on behalf of their threatened liberties. And when the other side says that there is nothing to be afraid of, again, if they are hard-hearted, their apparent lack of sympathy stems from their efforts to protect the fabric of society. Show of emotions is the supplementary arsenal in the war of words, as the faces of the protagonists in Christian Brunner's cartoon depict (see Figure 7).

This line of reasoning makes nonsense of attempts to find a basic human attitude toward risk and loss. But it is not cynical. There is nothing intrinsically wrong with the political contest being couched in terms of risk. It must be good that the voice of conscience is loud and clear, and right that those who are responsible for damage should be held to account. It is also right that the balance should be held between the contesting parties and that someone should speak on behalf of compromise and reconciliation. This is the crucial question of our times. There are reasons for not being sanguine about the outcome. One is that we have a culture that has evolved so as to minimize the risks of cultural conflict, to prevent it coming into the open, and that has somehow managed not to know that culture is inherently adversarial. In ignorance, we are likely to stir up strife inadvertently, and to be in danger of delivering unintended insults, provoking violence, and then, hearing the popular call for reprisals, following the path to serious civil discord.

Figure 7. The dialogue of the deaf. *Source:* Brunner 1989: 13.

RELIGIOUS FUNDAMENTALISM

Recognizing the importance of contemporary fundamentalism
and how little it is understood, the American Academy of Arts and
Sciences commissioned Martin E. Marty and R. Scott Appleby in
the Divinity School of the University of Chicago to organize the
Fundamentalism Project, enrolling an international panel of
scholars and publishing the results in several volumes (1991,
1993a, 1993b, 1994, and 1995), which are a superb resource for
studying religious enclaves. That the topic has contemporary
importance can be judged from the editors' bold introductory
paragraph to the volume entitled *Fundamentalism and Society:*

> In the early 1990's, pondering the collapse of communism
> across eastern Europe and the unraveling of Marxist ideology

> even in the Soviet Union, many American political commen-
> tators began to speculate: Whence will come the new enemy?
> Who or what will replace the "evil empire" as the focus of
> American reaction and enmity? What ideology, fortified by
> military, economic, or political power, will be virulent and
> contagious enough to challenge the efforts of liberal Western
> democracies to direct the course of global development?
>
> "Religious fundamentalism" was the answer that came
> from many quarters. (Marty and Appleby 1993a: 1)

These words imply that fundamentalism is itself in danger of
angry attack from the liberal democracies. But Marty and
Appleby go on to suggest the opposite, that it is, rather, the
Western democracies that are liable to attack from the fundamentalists. The end of the cold war was expected to lead, "in
Europe at least, to a new factionalism, to sectarian strife and violent ethnic particularisms, to skirmishes spilling over into border
disputes, civil wars, and battles of secession" (Marty and Appleby
1993a: 1). They list armed conflicts in 1991 in Yugoslavia,
Czechoslovakia, and the Baltic republics and threats of conflict
or outright conflict in India, Afghanistan, Sri Lanka, the Sudan,
and Nigeria. This introduction shows that the topic is by no
means a fusty academic issue but a live issue, and that fundamentalism is potentially extremely dangerous to peace is amply documented by various of the important essays that follow.

The editors take fundamentalism to be "a habit of mind found
within religious communities and paradigmatically embodied in
certain representative individuals and movements," the habit
manifested in a strategy to preserve distinctive identity as a people or a group; "feeling this identity to be at risk in the contem-

porary era, these believers fortify it by a selective retrieval of doctrines, beliefs, and practices from a sacred past" (Marty and Appleby 1993a: 67). If the identity includes total dissent from all of the claims of the surrounding society, the feeling of being at risk is probably well founded.

The "Western Academy" usually takes no notice of its detractors, but the editors of the Fundamentalism Project observe that they are everywhere opposed on principle by religious fundamentalists (Marty and Appleby 1993b: 5). We notice that even while priding themselves on objectivity and fairness and while demonstrating both in the published essays, they betray a bias by the selection and definition of the topic. Why do they separate the religious sects from other enclaves? Why look to emotions to explain religious behavior? Sectarianism is implicitly treated as a form of deviance, to be explained by an experience of deprivation that forces the person out of conventional behaviors.

William McNeil is one of many who maintain that fundamentalist movements are caused by deprivation. He is fully aware that it will be difficult to defend physical or economic deficiencies for unleashing the powerful commitment of fundamentalism, but he is apparently convinced that the cause is to be sought in deprivation of the old social structures that once provided security and confidence to peasant society. New forms of communication and population growth bring massive disruption, "creating personal uncertainty, isolation, and disappointment, more often than not. Resulting distress can and often does find expression in fundamentalist movements" (McNeil 1993: 561). Eloquent in favor of stability, he is nostalgic for the age-old frameworks of peasant and village life and sympathetic about their collapse in the face of forced entry to an exchange economy.

In the next breath he almost defeats his case by admitting that fundamentalism sometimes comes from the middle sectors of society. It is "rooted not in rural poverty and frustration or in the slums of Third World Cities, but in the comparative ease and luxury of professional and urban life." We are invited to feel sorry for the loneliness of the well-to-do, deprived of "the village solidarity and moral community which their parents both enjoyed and chafed at" (McNeil 1993: 566). McNeil recognizes that these movements are likely to increase in importance as the same destructive pressures mount against the moral community, but he takes an optimistic long view.

It is a pious hope which forgets that sects are inherently oppositional and factious. Enough of morality and emotions, and enough of classifying institutions according to religious commitment. If we want to understand fundamentalism we should try to fit it into the general cultural type that the form of organization indicates. Then other questions about enclavism will occur to us, questions that were not even posed in the religious perspective. For example, why are so many fundamentalists "People of the Book"? Why do they make important decisions by consulting the Book?

PROBLEMS OF ENCLAVISM

It is generally agreed that fundamentalists are exclusive groups, closed in the sense that transactions with nonmembers are restricted. Their exclusivity puts them at the extreme end of the dimension of group, the far right of the diagram, but it does not tell us whether to put them near the top. Second, we note that their burning thirst for justice and their anger against injustice, the emotions we know about from what they say, are embodied in egalitarian forms of organization. Being antithetical to hierarchical ranking, hereditary principles, and bureaucratic classification, enclaves belong in the bottom right corner of the diagram, in company with some nonreligious, paramilitary units—with the Provisional Irish Republican Army, for example. Third, enclaves are what Lewis Coser calls "greedy institutions" that try to preempt the total personality of their members, their time, and their resources. Coser explains institutional greediness by reference to their small size: "the exclusive group, being unable to avail itself of the advantages of large numbers, must attempt to offset it by the intensive exploitation of the loyalty of its members" (Coser 1974: 104), and it is true that the small group can have disadvantages of scale, but, as we shall see in the next chapter, many sociologists claim that small is better.

In brief: First, exclusivity; second, greed for control over the lives of members; from this derives hostility to outsiders, which leads to intolerance and refusal to negotiate, conspiracy theory, expulsions, and violence and the rest of sectarian behavior. But wait, does not this list have the priorities wrong? Why are some groups exclusive? Does not this have to be explained first?

Some would explain it by the principle of general dissent on which the group has been formed. Other groups can be critical and reformist without turning themselves into sects. The difference is the nature of their objectives. If they are a group of Victorians working together for a limited objective, to get the Corn Laws repealed or to abolish slavery or to introduce universal suffrage, they expect success to follow networking with others; so, far from becoming exclusive, they parley, they make temporary coalitions, and they keep patching up their longer-term amalgamations (Hollis 1974). By contrast, the sect is a minority whose dissent is total and which for that very reason has little expectation of realizing its objectives by normal means. The totality of its disagreement with the surrounding society draws it toward other means, hoping to succeed either because of miraculous interventions or by desperate violence.

The small, left-wing, extremist political group in London that Steve Rayner studied in the 1970s was a closed group in the full sense. Members of the group considered it both pointless and contaminating to talk to capitalist flunkies such as the Labour Party. The millennium would come of its own accord as soon as Mao Tse-tung judged the time ripe for a high-technology strike that would pulverize his enemies and restore freedom and justice to Britain (Rayner 1982). Their dissent was certainly total, they expected a miracle, but they were not religious.

But wait again! If total dissent leads to exclusivity, how are we to account for total dissent? To explain persons who regard themselves as hostile visitors to this planet, are we back to disappointment, frustration, anger, love of justice, or those mysterious, peculiarly religious, emotions? No, the emotions may be there, but they explain nothing.

Cultural theory assumes that an enclave constitution is a reasonable response to specific organizational problems. Characteristic solutions are offered, and when the key decisions are made they have cumulative effects on the original organization. No one person or group makes the important decision to turn it into an enclave culture; still less does the culture impose constraints on the individual members. The process of becoming an enclave is more like a slithering movement, from one decision to another that seems to be entailed by the first, or at least is made easier by the first having been taken. For a group to transform into such a system, it has to have chosen at least three of several courses: measures for closure, measures to prevent defection, and any of a range of measures to install egalitarianism. None of these courses alone would lead it to sectarianism. Only when all three are installed will its other future choices be locked into a sectarian framework. Taking the key decisions one by one, we can see how they implicate each other and how, once in place, they make a strong frame for a distinctive cultural bias.

First, why would a movement forgo the advantages of coalitions and close itself off? An experience of rejection, a calculation of futility, realistic recognition of incompatibility, responsibility for a unique cultural inheritance—there are plenty of good reasons for starting the process in a small way, adopting a distinctive name, refusing to get involved in other people's quarrels, and so on. Just being a cultural minority is enough to start down that path. This is going to be the beginning of the sense of persecution and the theory of conspiracy that marks the favored explanations.

Second, why would a movement take measures to stop defection? The answer is so obvious that the question seems silly. Most other kinds of movements use rewards and penalties, honors they can shower on their good members or withdraw from defaulters. The dissenting minority that tries to do any of these finds that it has few such resources: Its principles forbid it access to the big rewards of the outside society, and the latter will not lend its police to coerce members to stay in the fellowship. The children are the most important future members. It is eminently understandable that the movement should choose to control its youth, to provide a special education, and to reinterpret knowledge so that it is compatible with the foundation story and moral principles. Particularly, it will wish its children to marry within the community. This is going to be a major source of trouble, and it starts the formulation of theories about the evil outside and the virtuous inside.

The internal challenge is going to come from the children. Their questions and rebellions raise the stakes. While they are asking why certain friends are said to be bad for them or why certain pleasures are forbidden, their elders step up the reasons with lists of virtues and vices. Whenever the little ones see a loophole they will exploit it, so they force the elders to lead exemplary lives. Justice and fairness are the final crunch, the test of legitimacy: When the elders inveigh against injustice in the outside world, their own practices come under severe scrutiny at home. Even if the society did not start out as egalitarian, the dissident movement will eventually adopt some form of equality as one of its main principles. This will work out as a principle that forbids differentiation and so ensures maximum ambiguity in relationships among insiders.

Then the three pillars of the sectarian culture are in place, in a modest way at first: The protective boundary is built, the threat of defection is recognized, and principles of equality, nondiscrimination, and resultant ambiguity are established. From these entirely intelligible beginnings the rest evolves. After this, every crisis serves to intensify the exigent demands of the enclave on its members (Douglas 1986a). No need to invoke religious faith, or special hardships or deprivations, or emotions, to understand why the institution has become so greedy. The egalitarian organization must stop the obvious unfairness of leaders' free riding on the sacrifices of followers, but in doing so it hampers its own internal coordination. The leaders have no authority, so they tend to blame the corruption of the outside society for their difficulties. The more they adopt the posture of defiance toward the outside, the less are they going to be able to obtain external recognition. Compromise becomes more unthinkable; negotiation, more impossible. The cycle whirls them more and more speedily toward complete closure.

DECISION MAKING

Now we can ask why religions that refer everything to a "Book" endure and become world religions. The Book has many roles, but in the context of the severe difficulties of organizing people who are committed to not being organized—that is, to total egalitarianism—it has a saving role for decision making. The rich documentation of fundamentalism says little about the weaknesses of the enclave's egalitarianism. Exceptionally, Emmanuel Sivan's comparative review of enclaves in Christian, Arab, and Israeli traditions attends to questions of empowerment and legitimacy:

> The enclave, to repeat, is predicated upon voluntary membership and upon the quality of the virtuous insiders (circumscribed by the grids of gender and age). Yet these characteristics, combined, produce an unintended consequence: they hamper decision making and render authority ambiguous. This is all the more acute, as formal ranking and differentiated remuneration tend to be shunned (or minimized) for fear of defection. Who is, then, to constrain whom? How will virtue be maintained and strife avoided? (Sivan 1995: 50)

To answer, Sivan points to the role of the authoritative sacred text that enables them to disperse authority and still make decisions without seeming to decide. The text requires a live interpreter, and the interpretation has to be done "in a manner that will introduce as little institutional hierarchy as possible into the enclave, and thus disrupt that cherished asset, the intrinsic equality of the insiders" (Sivan 1995: 50). Sometimes a great reputation for scholarship is required for the post, sometimes otherworldly holiness and asceticism, or power of personality and rhetorical skills.

Hierarchical decision making is a favorite joke, for the bureaucrat goes by the book of procedural rules, however weakly they apply to the case in hand. Business uses so-called rational decision making, with a calculus for weighing all the relevant factors and coming up with the most effective or most economical solution. Enclaves have another method: consulting a book, but not the book of procedural rules. The Sacred Book can be treated like an oracle, consulted at random, giving guidance in the first lines at the top of the page. There are other ways of coming to a decision without involving authority—by casting lots, for example. Decision making by lottery is a much-underestimated and unstudied system. It reveals a legitimate course of action where there is no argument to justify a principle of choice. Like conventions, it only works when the persons involved want a decision so badly that they do not mind too much what it is. Administrative skills work the system by funneling the wide range of choices to a few, any of which will be acceptable to the persons involved.

Representing an enclave culture internationally is the least enviable job in the world. Enclave leaders have much less real authority than they seem to command. They are acutely aware of their own precariousness and can only be sure of carrying the people with them for popular commands. This predicament not only makes decision making difficult, it changes the content of what can be decided. It is easier to achieve a consensus for negative policies against the outsiders than to legislate for the inside, always riven with intrigues and unbridled rivalries. It is easier for an enclave leader to call for an attack than a cease-fire and easier to call for a cease-fire than make it effective.

INCIPIENT ZEALOTRY

It is tempting to smile at the predicaments of leaders at all times, and the predicaments of enclavist leaders are the worst. But let us remember that cultures are dynamic and ever shifting.

This is how zealotry develops. Wherever there are institutions, there is the possibility of solving problems by closure, and wherever that happens, enclavism is on the threshold. Sivan has found the typical enclavist attitude toward defection in religions that seem not to be at all enclavist on the surface (Sivan 1995). Christians, even apparently hierarchical Roman Catholics, once they start to close their group against outsiders, turn to worrying about losing their flock; the next stage is to start smelling traitors and denouncing conspiracies. Their doctrines become less liberal and their manners ruder, for all that they carry liberal and even hierarchist banners.

The enclave appeals powerfully to the young. When we remember that new sects are basically youth movements we can understand why they are so threatening to their opponents. They exert the pied-piper effect which the society that they are challenging has good reason to fear. The elderly hierarchists who are tempted to exert domestic authority have as much cause to worry about losing control of their young to the enclave as the enclave has reason to worry about losing its young to the glittering material power of the outside world. The same holds for the well-heeled individualist who has striven so hard to make his little pile: He wants respect from his family. It is difficult to hear his positivist ideals attacked in the name of a brand-new religion or an exotic Eastern mystical philosophy. Enmity is implanted between the cultures by their parallel problems of control and recruitment. The situation is explosive, and the times can become very interesting.

CHAPTER EIGHT

Shackled by Institutions

Personalities and ideas receive plenty of space in the study of religions, but religious institutions are neglected. In this chapter we will see that the whole topic of institutions is subject to heavy cultural bias. Our interest is in what happened to the idea of the person and, at this point, to the idea of the person in the theory of institutions. As that theory developed, it reflected the polarization of economics and sociology. In economics the individual emerges unfettered. He pleases himself, and how he does so is the data for an elaborate theory of consumption, whereas the different types of intervening institutions receive little attention. In sociology the individual tends to be seen as shackled by institutions, even threatened by them.

HISTORICAL INSTITUTIONALISM

In the nineteenth century when the burning question had been, "How should the study of society be conducted?" institutionalism and economic science came to be polarized around method. Classical economics was developing as a deductive science, and some economists were dissatisfied with its formalism and over-abstraction. Too much of social life and human concern, they considered, was allowed to slip through the meshes of economic analysis. In Germany an important school of "historical institutionalism" was founded, with a deliberately historical perspective and more descriptive as to method than was economics proper. Wilhelm Georg Roscher (1817–1894) founded the Historical School in protest against the deductive methods of classical economics. Political economy was to be approached by a careful historical analysis, taking the whole of society into its purview. This was overtly a methodological disagreement, but the difference over methodology traced back to disagreements about values.

The definition of rational behavior was the problem. When Utilitarianism defined rational behavior as self-interested, rational behavior became a target for criticism from Christians and from non-Christian idealists. Georg Roscher, himself a devout Protestant, proposed a model of self-interest that included human conscience as the regulator of desires. The leader of the "younger historical school," Gustav von Schmoller (1838–1917), was the foremost economist of imperial Germany. He also was strongly opposed to the abstract axiomatic-deductive approach of classical economic theory. His platform attacked three foes: Marxism, Manchester Liberalism, and reactionary views against social reform. It could be argued whether the movement went into decline because of its glorification of the Prussian state or because the massive volumes of historical work on particular industries or topics remained theoretically incoherent. Their rejection of formal argument and strict analysis would always have been a weakness, the more so because it split the subject of economics into two opposed camps, the theoreticians and the historians. Eventually the theoreticians of classical economics forged ahead on mathematical muscle; outside Germany, institutionalism was marginalized in the corners of economics departments and seemed to fade away.

Classical economics concentrated on market processes and paid scant attention to other institutions; at the same time, its methods became polarized against other branches of the social sciences. It even became necessary much later for Talcott Parsons to insist on the fact that the market depended on normative institutions in order to function at all (Parsons 1960). Partly because economics has a function in supplying interpretation and accurate information to industry and government, it has needed to develop refined analytical tools and a specialized language and lexicon. Though this rigor benefited economic theory, it was to the unintended detriment of related subjects that developed with less rigor, partly because the formalism had exclusionary effects, like a learned language which only the elite can speak, and partly, as was widely asserted, because the formal axiomatization left out so much of what was needed in the economic analysis and treated all relevant institutions as if they were a typical firm.

Eventually the academic discussion of institutions left economics and was relegated to history and sociology departments. Or you could say that the study of institutions left the marketplace and went to the outposts. The more effectively economics developed its own professional standards and became ever more strictly theoretical and deductive, the more it became the aristocrat among the social sciences and the more the study of institutions became peripheral and reactive. As cultural theory would predict for anything that goes into the margins and starts to close itself off, the course on institutions became the favored site for expressing moral indignation. The mood had a long history.

SHACKLED BY INSTITUTIONS

The history of institutions in the social sciences is riven with passionate arguments in which religious and political principles always lie not far below the surface. Preference for a method, deductive or inductive, is not just a choice about how to do it but a whole political attitude. From the turn of the century the French philosophers have been fairer to institutions, recognizing that some are the guarantors of civic liberties (Benjamin Constant and Alexis de Tocqueville; see Kelly 1992). At that stage the English thinkers wanted a theory that would protect the market's free operations from central institutions, while the French wanted to protect institutions from revolutionaries and anarchists. Their worry about instability was another political bias, one that made them less attracted to the anti-institutionalist bias we are describing.

Herbert Spencer had believed that the grand evolutionary movement of human society has been to free individuals from institutions that denied them security of property rights. To declare that the evolutionary arrow points toward private property was to aim a blow against socialism and Marxist social criticism, a blow against larger institutional control and for individual freedom. Early theories defending property rights tended to place the individual in opposition to legal and other constraints that might weaken his rights of possession. But always it is the same individual person, devoid of distinguishing features, homogenized, empty.

In the United States, Clarence Ayres (1891–1972), influenced to some degree by Thorstein Veblen, saw institutions as the enemy of progress. For Ayres, social development was synonymous with technological development; he was an evangelist preaching that technology was to institutions as spirit is to matter. Institutions are merely the ceremonial component of human behavior, like "flesh" and "vanity" in the old-time religion (Samuels 1988: 45–57). The study of institutions was a program of conscience, and institutions came out of it condemned as the source of society's ills.

Admittedly, the United States had another tradition of institutional economics (Seckler 1975), one that was fair to institutions. John Commons's (1862–1945) political view was that capitalist market forces needed to be modified by institutions which should provide a liberating framework for individual enterprise. And there still is contemporary institutionalist theorizing that takes individual property rights as the principle unit of analysis and their defense as its objective (Buchanan 1993).

After World War I sociological interest in institutions characteristically centered on the causes of social integration and disintegration. But it was more concerned with the negative effects of routinization than with the internal structure of various types of institutions or with the comparison of their diverse functionings. Archeological evidence of ruined ancient empires showed that elaborate institutions could produce total disintegration of a social system. This was made into a moral lesson against ambitious institutions. Sociology was worrying about blocked innovation, empty ritualism, and failure to develop adequate institutional solutions to new problems. Whereas large-scale institutions are proven to be every bit as sinister as anyone at the time could have suspected, the pity was to have put the problems they raise into the straitjacket of a general struggle of persons against institutions.

After nearly a century of denigration it is difficult for sociologists to think coolly about institutions. Anyone must notice that institutions are a bad word in Anglo-Saxon sociology, and even more so in psychology. Mysteriously, *structuration* and *networks* are acceptable, but *institution* and *routinization* are poisoned words. Institutions used to be seen essentially as ordered patterns that routinize behavior. Parallel to the economists' fear that monopoly hinders free trade, sociologists were seeing human intentions as thwarted by dysfunctioning institutions that inhibit progress, brutalize the growing child, and stunt the adult mind.

Admittedly important sociologists were teaching that institutions provide the normative framework of social life. Talcott Parsons (1937) made it a central feature of his teaching, but he turned it toward the relationship between institutions and moral sentiments, which he considered to be inculcated in childhood. Values and value-commitment were central themes in the social theory of Talcott Parsons in the 1930s to the 1950s (Parsons 1937, 1951, 1964).

This may be why Parsons was interested in Durkheim's theory of suicide (Durkheim 1968), in which Durkheim developed the concept of anomie, or normlessness. It became the only part of Durkheim's theory of mind and society that caught on in American sociology. Durkheim had taught that in complexly differentiated institutions moral commitment is weaker and that anomie characterizes modern society. Taking its cue from here, the sociological theory of institutions went on to study the moral dispositions that were supposed to keep an institution in place. The prominent issue was social disintegration due to alienation and lack of moral commitment, which would end by desiccating the proper life of institutions.

Though it might have been more to the point to have worried about the desiccation of sociology, it would not have been easy to shift gears. Peter Wagner describes how, after World War I, "the discourses of classical sociology proved increasingly inadequate for an understanding of state and society in transformation" (Wagner 1991: 238). He believes that this was partly because the problems of reconciling individual liberties with social cohesion had been analyzed in classical sociology (by Weber, Pareto, and Durkheim), and the predicted transformation into a bureaucratically administered mass society with organized capitalism had actually come about. In the new form of society the "discourse of classical sociology lost its cognitive affinity to the structure of the society which it dealt with" (Wagner 1991: 239).

We particularly notice that very little was being said about persons in relation to institutions. In the functionalist period, the 1950s and 1960s, sociological theory focused on roles and role performance. Persons in all their cultural variety were homogenized into one kind of rational being, and the central question was whether they were able to exercise their common rationality while performing in their standardized roles. Alvin Gouldner reproached role theory for treating the members of an institution as passive, likened to docile sheep obeying the barks of the institutional shepherd dog (Gouldner 1971).

With the political upheavals of the 1970s a radical change of direction seemed to draw attention to individual behavior. But sociologists were still discussing conformity, ritualism, deviance, and alienation (Riesman 1950). Social psychologists examined processes of socializing and how routinization suppresses the fragile psyche. Institutionalization was held to be destructive to personal autonomy. Processes of socialization and education were studied, so that schools could protect children from the insidious attack on personality.

By the end of the 1960s a romantic disenchantment held sway. Human nature was seen to be at risk from institutionalization (Goffman 1968). James Coleman even compares the social structures of ancient times, in which persons were the elements and "primordial ties" the basic relations, the "natural social environment," whereas the new social structure, in which corporate actors have come to take over many of the functions of primordial ties, is a "constructed social environment," in which streets and buildings displace forests and rivers! (Coleman 1990: 610). Sociology was discreetly marking solidarity with the egalitarian critics of society, the freedom fighters, the holy sectarians, the fundamentalists, and the other dissenting minorities. Humans are born equal, but everywhere they are in institutions—alas!

Brian Turner presents Talcott Parsons in the 1950s as treading a narrow path to defend American civilization, threatened on the right by McCarthyist movements and on the left by Russian communist power blocs (Turner 1991: xxxvii). Being caught in a political dilemma may explain the high moral tone and the political blandness. But it would be naive to suppose that the discipline instituted to reflect upon society could avoid bias. The surveys of the social sciences edited by Peter Wagner and his col-

leagues show with power and subtlety how ideology always inter-
penetrates with academia and public policy, both in the United
States and in Europe (Wagner, Weiss, and others 1991; Wagner,
Wittrock, and Whitley 1991). Two mainstream sociologies, the
pure academics of sociology, literary, speculative, and metaphysical, and another sociology with a talent for quantification, were
dedicated to the training of civil servants, welfare officials, statis-
ticians, and survey analysts. There came a point when there were
more sociologists outside the universities than in them (Wagner
1991: 237). Eventually, within sociology there were two cultural
biases that plotted easily on the cultural map (Figure 3): one culture teaching that the individual needs to be rescued from institutions and the other, a culture of the practitioners, paid by the
said institutions for which they provided quantitative data and
presumably not so bothered about the fate of the shadowy representative individual of their statistics.

On two fronts, then, by economists and by sociologists, institutions were flagged as a source of danger. But in spite of so much
interest, institutions themselves were relatively neglected. Different kinds of institutions were classified according to scale: like
predators, the larger, the more dangerous. As to their functioning and to how their internal structure contributed to their performance, the focus was crudely drawn on top-down–bottom-
up lines, rather than on lateral or other dimensions. Questions
about how different kinds of institutions exert control on individuals were only superficially treated. As there was one kind of
person, with the cultural differences smoothed out, so there
tended to be, and even to this day in organization theory there
still tends to be, one kind of organization with internal differen-
tiating structures smoothed out.

THE NEW INSTITUTIONALISM

In this context, a really New Institutionalism was not likely to emerge except from within economic theory itself. We now have an attempt to unify different branches of the social sciences, particularly to include economic theory, sociology, and history in one field. You can even say that economists had to launch a New Institutionalism because nothing positive was being taught about institutions. They won the initiative because the others, instead of making substantive comparisons of institutions as such, confined their interest to the harmful effects of institutions on individuals.

Inevitably, after the passage of nearly half a century, the new movement does not pick up where the old historical institutionalism left off. Nor do problems of personal identity and commitment, which were at one time so much at the fore in sociology, dominate the new theory of institutions. The image of the person passively victimized by oppressive institutions has been replaced by the idea that individuals are actually at work shaping their institutions according to a series of rational calculations.

The New Institutionalism is still interested in continuity and change, stagnation, innovation, and transmission of values, but methods and models have changed. Society is presented as an information system, and statistical regression analysis is still used, but the dominant concept is cybernetic. Kenneth Boulding had introduced the first model of society as a cybernetic feedback system in 1956.

Such a fast-developing field has many different strands. Geoffrey Hodgson has simplified the comparisons that could be made by distinguishing within institutional economics, a genuinely new one that takes the individual as the utility-maximizing being of economic theory and a new version of the old institutional economics, which is interested in individual commitment to moral values and cultural loyalties (Hodgson 1993). Each is a cultural bias in the sense we have been proposing, and each has a different theory of the person living inside the institutions and a correspondingly different policy solution. According to the first, institutional design can help to solve the problems of the environment and economic development by introducing economic incentives, such as road pricing, pollution tax, and so on, that appeal to the self-interest of individuals. According to the second, which has an evolutionist theoretical interest, there is a case for designing institutions to encourage social commitment and trust (Nelson and Winter 1982).

The two positions plot directly on the cultural map we introduced in chapter 5 (Figure 3). They represent the universal town meeting, the main two sides in an ongoing policy debate about the constitution. The choice between one or the other is not technical but political in the profoundest sense. In the case of the global environment the stage is not the town meeting but the globe. The confrontation is not at all trivial or academic. Institutions may not have been designed for that purpose, but in practice they embody moral principles. This makes the link between culture and the rational individual. The contestants in the constitutional debate must learn to discriminate between cultures according to the distinct constitutional goals from which they derive.

We are back to the hundred-year-old divergence between historical institutionalism and economics. On the one hand, the neoclassical economics' version of institutionalism has rational, self-interested individuals and powerful tools for analyzing their choices, but it has no space for culture. On the other hand, the new evolutionism has nice people with moral values, established habits, and useful routines—in other words, intelligent social beings endowed with culture. Those who feel drawn to the side of the nice people cannot but regret that the new evolutionist position is weaker theoretically. The new evolutionalism has no formal analysis equivalent to the rational-choice calculation, and it cannot identify how the preferred cultural values are held or transmitted. Both approaches need to allow for the capacity of rational individuals to respond to the structure of incentives that institutions provide.

Many New Institutionalists trace their start to Ronald Coase (1937), who wrote about the cost of transactions in business decisions. The problem for economists had been not so much that institutions were defined as peripheral to the market but that they seemed to be unamenable to the economists' methods of measurement and analysis. Coase saw that transaction costs could be analyzed according to the principle of substitution at the margins. Immediately this made institutions amenable to economic analysis, so that they are now accepted by economists as the complementary background of the market. (It would be unfair to suggest that leading sociologists and economists did not know this all along, but, as we explained in chapter 2, the information made no difference until it could be turned into a tool.)

Transaction costs add to the price of the product, in the same way as transport costs do. For the market to work well, information has to be freely available, yet for individual traders information about the market can be very expensive, to say nothing of the costs of negotiating and concluding contracts and monitoring how well the terms are observed. Economists now turn to the structure of institutions to explain the size of firms and the pattern of incentives. Baffling instances of economic stagnation become intelligible when the institutional structure is revealed.

The New Institutionalism puts paid to psychologizing about passive personality. It is true that some people accept being directed by others, let others carry risks for them, and tell them what to do: A whole industry of publications used to attribute their attitude to personality deficiency, laziness, cautiousness, a lack of entrepreneurial qualities. The new answer refers to the state of the market: Intelligent individual traders can recognize when the state of the market involves high transaction costs for the lone operator. The choice to enter a firm rather than remain as individual traders in the market is like other economic decisions. When uncertainty prevails, when security is expensive, when short-term contracts are difficult to negotiate and reliable information is at a premium, it pays to reduce a series of separate contracts to one—a contract of employment (Williamson 1975). This sounds as if it is sometimes intelligent for small firms to fold up and for their staff to sign on in larger ones. Oliver Williamson's approach was a landmark for a theory of individual opportunism and for cultural effects of organizations of different kinds. He allows us to consider effects of scale without an imported moral judgment.

SMALL AND PRIMITIVE

Histories of anthropology tend to account for the discipline's origins by reference to services rendered by its practitioners to colonial empires. But anyone can see that the information they supplied was not all that useful. Anthropology must have had something more to offer. A likelier candidate for sponsoring its beginnings is the role played by the imaginary primitive society in the early debates about the free market.

Herbert Spencer and other social evolutionists took encouragement from the continued existence in contemporary times of peoples who had not developed writing, differential calculus, or monetary instruments of exchange. The fact that these peoples had in their civic culture a large public sphere and a small private sphere was made relevant to arguments about private property. The individual could not be a true person without an enlargement of the private sphere. The idea of a starting point of human society in an unevolved, undifferentiated primitive society was a crucial element in their evolutionary theory.

Here we are again, back to the conundrums of our first chapter. The case of "primitive society" supports two moral lessons. One is that there, in ignorance and penury, would we be too if we did not actively protect our constitutions and promote our technology. The other is that we too should live in primitive simplicity: Here are people with limited wants, enjoying natural affluence and cultivating peace and harmony together. These contradictory assumptions still lurk in the writings of New Institutionalists, but our chances of sorting it out are better now. The Other, once the Primitive Other, is not just an illustration of a theme but a real existence, and we now know that our fates are bound together.

Some favorite fallacies are due to be dismantled as the movement updates its arsenal. One is the idea that transaction costs would be more easily brought under control in a small-scale society. The old institution bashing has been dressed up in new clothes. Michael Taylor (1982), supported by Douglass North (1990), believes that smallness of scale enables communities to overcome the difficulties of cooperation that beset larger ones.

He believes that in a simple, small-scale community, coordination problems can be solved more easily and that smallness of scale allows a community to achieve coordination by warm feelings of *Gemeinschaft*—another case of emotion doing service for explanation. Why should smallness make for warmth? What about sibling rivalry? The plug for smallness and simplicity is another swipe against institutions. Taylor thinks that where norms are well understood and members can make reasonable guesses about each other's beliefs, they will be able to agree with each other.

If the New Institutionalists are correct in thinking that cost-free information makes for economic efficiency, then a small-scale, simple community that enjoys zero transaction costs ought to be able to engage in complex trade and economic growth. But how could they stay small-scale in that event? Furthermore, it is not plausible that transaction costs would be under control in a small-scale society. Quite the opposite: The temptation to take a free ride on the efforts of others is as lively in small communities as in large. The unpleasantness and loss of popularity for monitoring and punishing are greater, the difficulty of holding anyone to his or her contract is overwhelming. All this inhibits the development of institutions the world over.

The opposite case is more defensible: In so-called primitive societies transaction costs are prohibitively high. The low level of economic development would be due to uncertainty, high risks, missing information about the intentions and beliefs of others, and high costs of monitoring and punishing defectors—in short, lack of the right kind of supporting institutions. Suppose a man in an African village asks someone to carry a valuable package to a distant creditor. How is he to prevent his messenger from absconding with the treasure? How can he keep his plans secret?

Even his own family, whom he is trying to support, is suspect. These are what the insurance industry calls moral hazards. When uncertainty is high and risks of cheating great, it makes sense to create "a community of fate" (Heimer 1985), so that the potential cheat sees his advantage in probity. Making the brother-in-law, nephew, wife, or sister a copartner engages some kin to share the costs of monitoring the other kin. It is rational for economy to be embedded in kinship, even though this is counterproductive for economic development.

The reasonable response to weak infrastructure—absence of insurance, lack of policing, unsafe highways, high information costs, low guarantees of honesty—is to embed trading activities in networks that produce increasing returns. More trust can be placed in family ties than in commercial relations: Investment in a kinship network of multiple obligations and long-term expectations will save on transaction costs. In this kind of society it is wise to be locked into protective institutions, to accept low-level and even restrictive cooperative solutions. The institutions in which economic activity is embedded serve multiple purposes: They protect children from abuse, old people from indigence, women from battering, as well as providing some general security for life and property. Lock-in has benefits as well as costs. It depends on the context.

THE EVOLUTION OF INSTITUTIONS

The fact that beliefs are held in common only signals that some coordination has been achieved, but it may well be very little—the limit of the possible—and, if so, it will surely rest on a precarious consensus (Douglas 1986a). We cannot infer the converse;

namely, that because of shared beliefs small-scale societies achieve a higher degree of coordination. Or why are they small scale?

They may be more hampered by transaction costs, but at some point we in the West managed to reduce them. The evolutionary question still stands. Contemporary evolutionism does not pick out a direction of development and then class all societies as successfully or unsuccessfully following it. Rather, it pays attention to the luck that attends an initial success. This is the concept of path-dependence and the related idea of dynamic increasing returns, and it is the effect of small random events (Arthur 1989). Evolution has returned to transform the history of innovation and technical development. Which of the two processes wins out depends not so much on which is the superior technology as on a run of luck that started a rolling snowball mechanism in favor of one.

> According to the cumulative technology theory, in the early history of automobiles, gasoline engines, steam engines, and electrical engines might all have been plausible alternative technologies for powering cars. While we now know that gasoline engines became dominant, according to this theory this might have been simply a matter of luck. By chance inventors tended to concentrate on it, or by chance big advances were made. However, once the gasoline engine had been developed to a point where it was significantly superior to extant steam or electrical engines, investing time and resources to advance these other technologies came to appear a bad bet, because such a large gap in performance needed to be made up before they would be competitive. (Nelson 1995: 74)

Nelson also applies the same argument to the evolution of institutional structures in industry linked to the evolution of technology.

The notion that institutions are put together piecemeal and episodically, by a mixture of chance and intelligent opportunism, not deliberately designed, not engineered, but strengthened by habit and convenience, may seem jejune and unexciting. However, that idea itself enjoys dynamic, increasing returns, because it fits with other current ideas about conventions and coordination problems. When there is a wish to solve a problem of coordination and no preference as to how it be solved, the convention that is most easily adopted is one which is easily recognized and which looks after its own policing. For example, driving on the right or the left side of the road is pure convention, and no one says that one is better than the other; but the local convention works because every road user wants there to be a convention, and it is self-policing because the other drivers show their fury in no uncertain terms against a car that is driven on the wrong side (Lewis 1969; Schelling 1978). Similarly, a particular day has to be adopted for holding markets, and once it is established, other institutions grow up around the decision, they all lock together so that it becomes difficult to change. Conventions explain path-dependency, increasing returns, and saving on transaction costs.

The new theoretical style is appealingly modest. It resonates sympathetically to a postmodern mood. When institutions are seen to be made in much the same cooperative but unplanned way as language is made, they appear less inimical to constitutional liberties. When institutions were cast in a more controlling role, they raised the question of sociological determinism. But now that institutions are seen to be somewhat haphazard in their origins, a patchwork of pressures and counterpressures, possibly dynamic, possibly static, the question of their influence on the minds of their members takes a different form.

Early institutionalists feared that their cherished social values would be submerged by the grandiose deductive models of classical economics. They objected to the hubris of formal deductivism and the concealed political bias in economics. Though they became unfashionable, the trend has come full circle with microeconomic studies and interest in conventions as the foundation of institutions. The new account of institutional change and resistance to change is theoretically minimalist. In the history of ideas path-dependence and economies in (intellectual) transaction costs can explain increasing returns from following a convention. We could say that the idea of convention begins to acquire increasing returns on its own account, as an idea, and becomes more intelligible and acceptable as it is taken up in one field after another.

A new round has begun. We suspect that one of the losers will surely be the idea of decision making. Critics describe the process as a ritual that hallows what has happened already. What has really happened is not a definite decision but first slithering a little way down the easiest path and then slithering further down the same path the next time a choice seems to be needed, because of all the advantages accrued to the way that has been begun. The theory of institutional evolution by small but highly consequential slithers would fit well to what we showed in chapter 7 about the growth of enclave cultures. A first move toward moral dissent, another move toward closure, then defection appears as a problem, another move to closure to defeat defection, and then all the familiar solutions present themselves, with the effect of tightening the outside boundary, vilifying the outside, bolstering virtue to justify the moral dissent. Almost irresistibly, the path of least resistance increases the attraction of full-scale enclavism.

The slither theory works just as well for the insidious shifts into bureaucracy and full-scale hierarchy. It works just as well for the moves that start with dismantling obsolete parts of established institutions and goes on to develop full-blown patronage systems based on individual negotiation. Cultural theory says that the almost indiscernible processes of choice exert a pull toward determinate institutional forms, but it does not say that an effort to stop and turn around must fail.

CHAPTER NINE

Homo Œconomicus:
A Way of Saying Nothing

If institutions are vehicles for moral purposes, as we understand, a difficult theoretical task lies ahead. We have to consider these vehicles as ways of living. The better to watch the interplay of moral purposes and institutions, we have chosen four types. The social being is exposed to the influence of other persons through these culture-bearing institutions. This makes the idea of a social person replete; each one is furnished with the code for transmitting and receiving signals from others; and as they use it they are changing the code. Instead of one we have several rational persons. Four kinds of rational beings, with four kinds of values, and each with three kinds of enemies: The missing persons have been reinstalled. But it is not at all clear that knowing about ourselves and our allegiances is going to make any difference to the way we live together. There seems to be a strong impulse to deny cultural difference and to avoid drawing attention to it, perhaps even to avoid thinking about it.

PREFERRING TO SAY NOTHING

As we saw in chapter 8, risk discourse allows the radical critics to talk about failures of democracy without undertaking a radical reexamination of the foundations of society. It is not that the task is intellectually too taxing, though that could always be a problem. More interestingly, it may be that living together in a plural democracy requires that strong opinions be muted. If this has been the underlying concern, the way that the topic of risk perception has developed over the past quarter century is less puzzling (Douglas 1986b; Douglas and Wildavsky 1983).

Perhaps, in modern, industrial democracy, anything that threatens to be radical is liable to be either neutralized or shunned. The risk discourse is a kind of sieve through which anger must pass to be purified. By the rigorous search for universal cognitive laws the psychometricians have achieved this pure status, above and beyond politics. Research on psychometric lines gave the halo of objectivity to a newly emergent profession, but the price the psychometricians are apt to pay is the vacuity of their results. The part that interests us here is the process of neutralizing. That it might be necessary to speak and to say nothing suggests another function for the empty person at the head of rational-choice theory. That may be the secret of *Homo œconomicus*, his resilience, his gift to democracy: to cover conflict and to enable us to live together.

There may have been a time when it was better not to look, better to pretend that politics could be excluded, but the cultural balance has changed. A whole new technology underpins our institutions and shifts the weight of our values. In these last pages we will develop our final point, which is that cultural theory enables us to confront our own political bias. We need not worry that it will wake the slumbering passions. As a contribution to self-awareness and as a mirror for reflexivity, it is too recondite to disturb the amenities of civil society. If at this point it is better to know about political emotions in a systematic way, this is a tool that can reveal them.

FOUR STRATEGIES OF CONTROL

The current interest in microprocesses is a good sign in our quest for the whole person. The theoretician who is interested in random small effects with large consequences and in unpredictable, dynamic increasing returns gives more room to real persons who are maneuvering and negotiating with other real persons. Following paths of least resistance is not irrational: Doing their modest best, the persons may merely hope to leave the conference table without too much discredit, or absentmindedly attach new territories to existing empires, or weakly declare war against their better judgment. This is the more realistic perspective of New Institutionalism. We can even reverse the alleged process by which institutions do things to people. We can expect people to do things to institutions; we can even design institutional rewards and penalties that will help other people to resist path dependency and fulfill the cultural purposes for which the institutions have been set up. Then we can expect them to put up with the design weaknesses for the good reason that it is more difficult to change the institutional design than to put up with it.

Our legacy of thinking about public administration has only one repetitive idea: Bureaucracy is hierarchical; hierarchies are

bureaucratic. When we have to think about how they are controlled, the first model that comes to mind is the inspectorate;
and when we think about how they become inept, we think of a
rule-bound superstructure, top-heavy with custodians checking
on other custodians and perversely committed to its own perpet-
uation rather than to its manifest tasks. Bureaucratic institutions
are supposed to go on too long, and when they collapse, they all
collapse from overweight. Evidently, institutions suffer the same
kind of stereotyping as do persons, and they would benefit from
cultural theory's map, which locates different kinds of institutions according to the values they support.

Christopher Hood (1996) has used cultural theory to examine
public administration. With his own cybernetic version of control
models he distinguishes four types of doctrine of good government and democracy. Summarizing briefly a complex argument,
his quartet of administrative controls is a set of four strategies or
devices.

The first he calls "contrived randomness." It is a form of administration whose objective is to prevent collusion, corruption, and
fraud and which does so by reducing the contacts between staff
members and by increasing unpredictability. In cultural-theory
terminology it combines a highly programmed structure—high
grid—with weak bonds—low group. By deliberately producing
inability to initiate or interact it creates a population of isolates
who do not know what is going on around them and who see no
rewards for cooperation: "Contrived randomness brings about
precisely this effect by making the operation of public administration organisation, and therefore the payoffs of cooperation among
those who work in or with it—as clients, purchasers, providers,
authorizers, as unpredictable as possible" (Hood 1996: 220). The

organizational design is typical of traditional bureaucracies and multinational companies, devised especially for controlling financial or field-group operations: It includes division of authority, limited tenure, rotation of staff, semirandom postings, unannounced random checks. What he calls the "fruit machine" model is notorious in the satirical fiction of mindless bureaucracy. Susan Rose-Ackerman, in her study of corruption (1978), calls this model "disorganized bureaucracy." She explains that it may keep down corruption because the key pressure points in a decision system are more difficult to identify in advance by extortionists or bribers. This type of organization produces the cultural bias of isolates elsewhere, fatalism, as marked on the cultural map in Figure 3.

Hood's next form of public administration control he calls "mutuality." This fits uncannily well and unexpectedly to the bottom right-hand corner of the same diagram, the place of egalitarian sects and communes. It is a collegial group process that is used to prevent individuals from acting alone and to keep each in harness with colleagues whose interest is to prevent corruption, as when police officers on patrol are paired, or in performance appraisal by colleagues or even by subordinates (the Chinese Cultural Revolution style, or peer review in academia, self-government, and other forms of peer group accountability). Making cooperation the central element of control strategy, groupism replaces chancism, with the effect of blurring boundaries between controller and controlled, insider and outsider. The current vogue for peer-group audits in the United Kingdom in the medical and university professions is an example of control by groupism. Hood points out darkly that, according to cultural theory—which argues that living with ambiguity causes strain—such systems survive only by continual expulsion of deviants or heretics. Yes! Does not this explain something we knew already but did not understand: the bitterness of academic infighting?

Third, Hood counts competition as a deliberate technique of public administration, which maps directly on the cultural map as individualism. He uses several examples of efforts to introduce into public administration competition for clients, or for customers, or among customers, for contracts.

Lastly, the more familiar control by oversight and review fits with the hierarchist cultural bias as placed on the cultural map and described in chapter 5. In organizations it involves establishing a ladder of authority and expertise and is clearly not compatible with the other forms of control.

A distinguished sinologist has remarked that it is exceedingly difficult for contemporary scholars to understand Chinese history and philosophy because of our difficulties with the idea of hierarchy (Schwartz 1985). As if to prove his point, one of Hood's examples is misclassified. He cites a classic portrayal of the "village world" of the top British civil service at the treasury (Heclo and Wildavsky 1974). It "depicts a system in which the behaviour of high-flying bureaucrats is controlled by continual exposure to the judgement and assessment of colleagues over a working life-time of forty years or so" (Hood 1996: 217). Hood takes it for an example of control by mutuality, setting peers to watch each other. But top civil servants who have been working together for all their lives were not all on top when they started; when they were beginners they were supervised by the then top bureaucrats, and for forty or more years, as they moved up the ladder, they have been buffered by seniority. Their assessment system has no interpersonal ambiguities and does not result in the blurring of lines between insiders and outsiders, between controllers and controlled, as happens with peer review in universities.

Though each seems to be completely antithetical to the other methods of control, the four systems can coexist as long as the areas of responsibility are well defined. Hood recognizes that each of these strategies for control can be found in different levels or compartments of a single administrative unit. He is good at describing how hybrid systems work and at showing where conflict between opposing principles may lead to weakness and breakdown. He concludes that precariousness and instability are predictable features of control systems in public management. He does not go so far as to predict different kinds of disequilibrium for the different cultural regimes, though this would be possible. He suggests that the cultural typology may be used to find the Achilles heel of the different forms of control.

INSTITUTIONS CONFORM
TO TECHNOLOGIES

In effect, what Hood describes so well as strategies of control are separate paths that lead toward dominant cultural types. In spite of what we said above about historical happenstance as the main principle of innovation, the different cultures do not become dominant by luck. Developing what we said in chapter 8 about the evolution of technology, a style of organization and its culture have a better chance of coming out on top if they suit the dominant technological type. A culture's fitness to survive in a firm or public administration would depend partly on how well its prevailing cultural atmosphere fits the prevailing technological conditions.

When one of these control strategies has been adopted, it

allows room for another of the same cultural color. If the relevant technology is correct, it provides a reason for going on in the same direction. It follows that the first form of failure which lies in wait for all four cultural types is the wrong institutional structure for the technological base.

Technological change in our day makes it possible to call the urbane formalism of *Homo œconomicus* into question. The technological base has changed; and with a new communications system involving dispersed authority and easy dissolution of ties, a new cultural regime has emerged. This is what is going to make it possible to do what was frowned on before: to examine ourselves and others in a fourfold reflecting mirror.

Enclave's weak or dispersed authority system does not flourish with centralized technology. To the extent that it is based on electronic communication, our own society has become friendlier ground for enclavism of all kinds. The enclave formula is good for effective defense of large principles and small groups. It is bad at budgetary control, because egalitarianism entails internal factions and weak authority (Wildavsky 1975, 1980). It is good for organizing short-term offensives. Enclave would flourish when the political conditions are against any realistic expectation that it will take over the government; when administrative impotence is guaranteed and the budget is controlled by the adversary, criticism can be unconstrained.

Clearly, a technology of communication by which accountability is globally dispersed would also be favorable to the culture of individualism, as in our great multinational corporations. This culture entails many great weaknesses. One is the lack of investment in public goods. Another is that its star performers can be bought by rivals. Another is the difficulty of justifying an effective theory of social justice in terms acceptable to *Homo œconomicus*. Another is the combination of moral weakness and military strength.

The same technological base encourages the culture of isolates. It allows individuals who voluntarily indulge a preference for privacy to evade groups that try to recruit them. And, at the same time, you would expect that conditions which favor individualism would also see a rise in the proportion of involuntary isolates, for several reasons. First, individualism is essentially competitive, and the more severe the competition in the top league, the less room there is at the top and the larger the population excluded from competing at all. Second, because individualism watches the costs and reckons a large umbrella of welfare to be too expensive to maintain, the greater the number of persons who have to make the best of it on their own.

In the sequence of cultural regimes, hierarchy has had its day. It can survive, but with scant respect and only in carefully protected niches. Nor is it any accident or mistake that has led to *institution* becoming another bad word. Hierarchy as the dominant form of control survives well where the technology of production encourages a strong command system. Hierarchy is good for heavy manufacturing industry, imperial wars, and wherever centralization is useful. It also provides a practicable form of justification for other centralized controls—the budget, for example (Wildavsky 1980). The advantage of a family budget is one reason why the gender and age–stratified family tends to be cited as an example of hierarchy (Boltanski and Thévenot 1991). Holding a far-flung colonial empire is easier when the same form of thinking applies to the production system, to the military, naval, policing, and administrative cadres, and to the family.

There are gains in credibility in being able to use the same rhetoric to justify measures taken at various levels, as Britain found in the eighteenth century. The work of clarifying the link between the technological base and the prevailing cultural bias, well begun by Schmutzer (1994), would go a long way toward anticipating responses to public policy.

When we have considered some of the (quite well-known) weaknesses of each cultural type, we ought to recognize that they also have their respective methods of compensating. For example, on the face of it their tendency to control knowledge ought to be a besetting weakness of both hierarchy and enclave. It may be dangerous for hierarchy because of the danger of not knowing when times are changed and administrative formulas are outdated. However, hierarchy makes capital out of the weakness by developing its own invincible microcosmic theory of the universe. Enclave, as a protest movement, is less dependent on being in touch with the times. It can afford to indulge in creationism and flat-earthism in science and in primitivism in doctrine. If it boasts an original, esoteric revelation, it can make a virtue of its strict control of knowledge. How else but by censorship can it preserve its legacy?

CONCLUSION

This is the time to pull together the various threads of our argument. The first and main point is that our culture at present gives us ample ways to reflect on ourselves as individuals, but not as cultural creatures. Where we would expect to find accounts of the person exercising the fullness of moral and political choice, we find a blank cipher. Utility theory shows the person as a choosing machine, but the choices are treated piecemeal. Their implications for a moral standpoint are overlooked, and heavier weight is put on the right of a person to stay alive than to live according to choice. We proposed that *Homo œconomicus* is like the microcosms of ancient civilizations, in which the body of a human, the body politic, and the celestial bodies are moved by the same universal principles.

We have tried to assess the strength of this microcosmic vision and some of the problems it poses, intellectual conundrums about poverty and collective choice, and practical dilemmas about dealing with other persons whose political behavior we cannot even start to understand. We have noticed some perverse effects. Here are social sciences, so-called, which proceed as if rational humans are not primarily social beings. The English language can make a plural out of the singular word, but the plural of *person* is more generally rendered as *people*, with the connotations of the root for popular, populace, population. The theoretical posture seems to be justified because it protects objectivity, yet it is no protection against subjective bias, as we observe when we see how heavily biased are the social sciences against institutions.

We have proposed that a theory of culture can remedy these shortcomings. It assumes a theory of rational persons fully empowered to espouse political and moral choices, able to choose to abide by them or choose to abandon them, according to circumstances. These choices sum up the predilections of a lifetime, past hopes dashed or expectations fulfilled. The political and moral choices are about how to live in society. One way of living rules out another, because each one must appropriate space and time and objects for the purposes it can achieve. So the choices do not come in random bundles or as separate disconnected items.

Is it worth the effort of trying to see through the veils of our own culture? Yes, it is worthwhile to develop a new theory of the person, because there are important issues that we cannot face squarely or fairly without a better concept of the human as a political animal. One of these is political conflict. Enclave culture is always with us, always protesting on behalf of justice, often living peacefully among the rest, not persecuted or arraigned, not violent, but sometimes driven to seething rage.

So much has been written about enclave cultures, in the intellectual vein of the humanities, about fundamentalist ideas, theories, histories, ideals. So little, in comparison, has been written about their organization. Yet their ideals are embodied in the typical institutions of people who have, for whatever reason, started to be exclusive. Inimical to hierarchists and individualists alike, the enclave culture is presented by outsiders as utterly alien and incomprehensible. But as we examine it more closely, we can almost see how the terrifying wild thing becomes domesticated. Here we are, practicing exclusion, closing our boundaries, worrying about defection when we ought to be able to see ourselves as we slide down the slope. Whether we see it coming or not, enclavism is always possible—often probable—and zealotry is not impossible.

Bibliography

Abensour, Miguel, ed. 1987. *L'Esprit des lois sauvages: Pierre Clastres ou une nouvelle anthropologie politique.* Seuil, Paris.

Ackerman, Bruce. 1980. *Social Justice in the Liberal State.* Yale University Press, New Haven, Conn.

Affichard, Joelle, and Jean-Baptiste de Foucauld, eds. 1995. *Pluralisme et équité: La Justice sociale dans les democraties.* Editions Esprit, Paris.

Allardt, E. 1975. *Att ha, alska, att vara: om valfard i Norden.* Argos, Borgholm, Sweden.

———. 1993. "Having, Loving, Being: An Alternative to the Swedish Model of Welfare Research." In Martha Nussbaum and Amartya Sen, eds., *The Quality of Life,* 88–94. Clarendon Press, Oxford.

Ardener, Shirley. 1975. *Perceiving Women.* Halstead Press, London.

Arthur, Brian. 1989. "Competing Technologies, Increasing Returns and Lock-in by Historically Small Events." *Economic Journal* 99 (393): 116–131.

Ayres, Clarence. 1938. *The Problem of Economic Order.* Farrar and Rinehart, New York.

———. 1952. *The Industrial Society.* Houghton Mifflin, Boston.

Bachrach, Peter, and Morton Baratz. 1962. "Two Faces of Power." *American Political Science Review* 56: 1947–1952.

———. 1970. *Power and Poverty.* Oxford University Press, New York.

Bastide, Roger. 1978. *The African Religions in Brazil.* John Hopkins University Press, Baltimore, Md.

Beck, Ulrich. 1992. *Risk Society: Towards a New Modernity.* Sage, London.

Becker, Howard S. 1963. *Outsiders: Studies in the Sociology of Deviance.* Free Press, New York.

Berger, Peter, and Thomas Luckmann. 1966. *The Social Construction of Reality: A Treatise in the Sociology of Knowledge.* Penguin, London.

Bernouilli, Daniel. [1738]. "Specimen Theoriae Novae de Mensura Sartis." *Commentarii academiae scientarum imperialis Petropolitanae* 5: 175–192. English translation by L. Sommer, "Exposition of a New Theory on the Measurement of Risk," *Econometrica* 22 (1954): 23–36.

Berreman, Gerald D., ed. 1981. *Social Inequality: Comparative and Developmental Approaches.* Academic Press, London.

Boltanski, Luc, and Laurent Thévenot. 1991. *De la justification: Les Économies de la grandeur.* Gallimard, Paris.

Boulding, Kenneth. 1956. *The Image: Knowledge in Life and Society.* University of Michigan Press, Ann Arbor.

———. 1970. *Economics as a Science.* McGraw-Hill, New York.

Bourdieu, Pierre. 1979. *La Distinction.* Editions de Minuit, Paris.

———, ed. 1993. *La Misère du monde.* Seuil, Paris.

Broderick, A., ed. 1970. *The French Institutionalists.* Harvard University Press, Cambridge, Mass.

Brunner, Christian, illustrator. 1989. In Serge Prêtre, *Nucléaire symbolisme et société: Contagion mentale ou conscience des risques?* SFEN, Paris.

Buchanan, James. 1993. *Property, the Guarantor of Liberty.* Edward Elgar, Aldershot, England.

Burke, Kenneth. 1950. *A Rhetoric of Motives.* Prentice Hall, Englewood Cliffs, N.J.

Burton, John, ed. 1990. *Conflict: Human Needs Theory.* St. Martin's Press, New York.

Caillé, Alain. 1986. *Splendeurs et misères des sciences sociales: Esquisses d'un mythologie.* Librairie Droz, Geneva.

———. 1989. *Critique de la raison utilitaire, manifeste du MAUSS.* La Découverte, Paris.

———. 1993. *La Demission des clercs, la crise des sciences sociales et l'oubli du politique.* La Découverte, Paris.

Clastres, Pierre. 1972. *Chronique des indiens Guayaki.* Plon, Paris.

Clifford, James, 1982. *Person and Myth: Maurice Leenhardt in the Melanesian World.* University of California Press, Berkeley.

Coase, Ronald. 1937. "The Nature of the Firm." *Economica* 4: 386–405.

Coleman, James. 1990. *Foundations of Social Theory.* Belknap Press of Harvard University Press, Cambridge, Mass.

Collingridge, David. 1992. *The Management of Scale: Big Organisations, Big Decisions, Big Mistakes.* Routledge, London.

Commons, John. 1934. *Institutional Economics.* Macmillan, New York.

Cornell, Stephen, and Joseph P. Kalt. 1992. "Cultures and Institutions as Public Goods: American Indian Economic Development as a Problem of Collective Action." In Terry L. Anderson, ed., *Property Rights and Indian Economies,* 46–68. Rowman and Littlefield, Lanham, Md.

Coser, Lewis. 1974. *Greedy Institutions: Patterns of Undivided Commitment.* Free Press, Collier Macmillan, New York.

Coyle, Dennis J., and Richard J. Ellis, eds. 1994. *Politics, Policy and Culture.* Westview Press, Boulder, Colo.

Dahl, Robert A. 1961. *Who Governs?* Yale University Press, New Haven, Conn.

Dake, Karl. 1991. "Orienting Dispositions in the Perception of Risk: An Analysis of Contemporary World Views and Cultural Biases." *Journal of Cross-Cultural Psychology* 22 (1): 60–81.

———. 1993. "The Meanings of Sustainable Development: Household Strategies for Managing Needs and Resources." In Scott D. Wright, ed., *Human Ecology: Crossing Boundaries,* 87–113. Society for Human Ecology, Fort Collins, Colo.

Danziger, Kurt. 1990. *Constructing the Subject: Historical Origins of*

Psychological Research. Cambridge University Press, Cambridge, England.

Dasgupta, Partha. 1993. *An Inquiry into Well-Being and Destitution.* Clarendon Press, Oxford.

Dawkins, Richard. 1976. *The Selfish Gene.* Oxford University Press, London.

Dennett, Daniel C. 1987. *The Intentional Stance.* MIT Press, Cambridge, Mass.

————. 1991. *Consciousness Explained.* Alan Lane, London.

Douglas, Mary. 1970. *Natural Symbols: Explorations in Cosmology.* Penguin, London.

————. 1986. *Risk Acceptability According to the Social Sciences.* Routledge, London.

————. 1987. *How Institutions Think.* Syracuse University Press, Syracuse, N.Y.

————. 1992a. "In Defense of Shopping." In R. Eisendle and E. Miklautz, eds. *Produktkulturen: Dynamik und Bedeutungswandel des Konsums,* 48–65. Campus Verlag, Frankfurt am Main, Germany.

————. 1992b. "Thought Style Exemplified: The Idea of the Self." In *Risk and Blame: Essays in Cultural Theory,* 211–234. Routledge, London.

————. 1993. "Emotion and Culture in Theories of Justice." *Economy and Society* 22 (4): 501–514.

————. 1995. "Justice sociale et sentiment de justice: Une anthropologie de l'inégalité." In Joelle Affichard and Jean-Baptiste de Foucauld, eds., *Pluralisme et équité: La Justice sociale dans les democraties,* 123–151. Editions Esprit, Paris.

————. 1996. "Prospects for Asceticism." In *Thought Styles: Critical Essays on Good Taste,* 161–192. Sage Publications, London.

————, ed. 1982. *Essays in the Sociology of Perception.* Routledge and Kegan Paul, London.

Douglas, Mary, and Baron Isherwood. 1979. *The World of Goods.* Basic Books, New York.

Douglas, Mary, and Aaron Wildavsky. 1983. *Risk and Culture: An Essay on the Selection of Technological and Environmental Dangers.* University of California Press, Berkeley.

Douglas, Mary, Des Gasper, Steven Ney, and Michael Thompson. 1998. "Human Needs and Wants." In Steve Rayner and Elizabeth L. Malone, eds., *Human Choice and Climate Change*, vol. 1, *The Societal Framework*, 195–263. Battelle Press, Columbus, Ohio.

Downs, A. 1967. *Inside Bureaucracy.* Little, Brown, Boston.

Drewnowski, J., and W. Scott. 1966. *Level of Living Index.* Report No. 4. United Nations Research Institute for Social Development (UNRISD), Geneva.

Dryzek, John S. 1993. "Policy Analysis and Planning: From Science to Arguments." In Frank Fischer and John Forester, eds., *The Argumentative Turn in Policy Analysis and Planning*, 213–232. Duke University Press, Durham, N.C.

Duclos, Denis. 1991. *L'Homme face au risque technique.* Harmattan, Paris.

Du Maurier, George. 1880. "The Six-Mark Teapot" [illustration]. *Punch, or The London Charivari*, 79 (October 30): 194.

Dunbar, R. I. M. 1989. "Social Systems as Optimal Strategy Sets: The Costs and Benefits of Sociality." In V. Standen and R. Foley, eds., *Comparative Socioecology*, 131–149. Blackwell Scientific Publications, Oxford.

———. 1995. *The Trouble with Science.* Faber and Faber, London.

Durkheim, Émile. 1968. *Suicide: A Study in Sociology.* Edited with an introduction by George Simpson. Routledge and Kegan Paul, London.

———. 1995 [1912]. *The Elementary Forms of Religious Life.* Translated by Joseph Ward Swain. Free Press, New York.

Durkheim, Émile, and Marcel Mauss. 1903. "De quelques formes primitives de classification: Contribution à l'étude des réprésentations collectives." *L'Année Sociologique* 6: 1901–1902. Reprinted in 1963 as *Primitive Classification*, translated by Rodney Needham, University of Chicago Press, Chicago.

Ellis, Richard, M. Thompson, and Aaron Wildavsky. 1990. *Cultural Theory*. Westview Press, Boulder, Colo.

Elster, Jon. 1982. "Sour Grapes: Utilitarianism and the Genesis of Wants." In A. K. Sen and B. Williams, eds., *Utilitarianism and Beyond*, 219–228. Cambridge University Press, Cambridge, England.

Erikson, R. 1987. *The Scandinavian Model: Welfare States and Welfare Research*. M. E. Sharpe, Armonk, N.Y.

Evans-Pritchard, E. E. 1937. *Witchcraft: Oracles and Magic among the Azande*. Clarendon Press, Oxford.

Fischer, Frank, and John Forester, eds. 1993. *The Argumentative Turn in Policy Analysis and Planning*. Duke University Press, Durham, N.C.

Fischhoff, B. 1990. "Psychology and Public Policy: Tool or Toolmaker?" *American Psychologist* 45: 647–653.

Foucault, M. 1980. *Knowledge/Power*. Harvester Wheatsheaf, London.

Freud, Sigmund. 1960. *Jokes and Their Relation to the Unconscious*. Translated and edited by James Strachey. W. W. Norton, New York and London.

Fried, Charles. 1970. *An Anatomy of Values*. Harvard University Press, Cambridge, Mass.

Galison, Peter. 1987. *How Experiments End*. University of Chicago Press, Chicago.

Galtung, Johan. 1990. "International Development in Human Perspective." In John Burton, ed., *Conflict: Human Needs Theory*, 301–335. St. Martin's Press, New York.

Genestier, Philippe. 1994. "Misérabilisme ou populisme? Une Aporie des sciences sociales." In *A qui se fier? Confiance, interaction et theorie des jeux. La Revue du MAUSS Semestrielle* 4 (2): 229–251.

George, Vic. 1988. *Wealth, Poverty and Starvation: An International Perspective*. Wheatsheaf Books, London.

Gigerenzer, G., and D. Goldstein. 1996. "The Mind as a Computer: The Birth of a Metaphor." *Creativity Research Journal* 9: 131–144.

Gigerenzer, Gerd. 1991. "From Tools to Theories: A Heuristic of Discovery in Cognitive Psychology." *Psychological Review* 98: 254–267.

————. 1992. "Discovery in Cognitive Psychology: New Tools Inspire New Theories." *Science in Context* 5 (2): 329–350.

Goffman, Erving. 1968. *Asylums: Essays on the Social Situation of Mental Patients and Other Inmates.* Penguin, Harmondsworth, England.

Gooding, David, T. Pinch, and E. S. Shaffer, eds. 1989. *The Uses of Experiment: Studies in the Natural Sciences.* Cambridge University Press, Cambridge, England.

Goodman, David, and Michael Redclift. 1991. *Refashioning Nature: Food, Ecology and Culture.* London, Routledge.

Goody, Esther, ed. 1995. *Social Intelligence and Interaction: Expressions and Implications of the Social Bias in Human Intelligence.* Cambridge University Press, Cambridge, England.

Gould, S. J. 1981. *The Mismeasure of Man.* W. W. Norton, New York.

Gouldner, Alvin. 1971. *The Coming Crisis of Western Sociology.* Basic Books, New York.

Grendstad, G., P. Selle, and K. Strømnes. 1996. "Natur og Kultur." In Gunnar Grendstad and Per Selle, eds., *Kultur som Levemåte,* 183–199. Samlaget, Oslo.

Grendstad, Gunnar, and Per Selle, eds. 1996. *Kultur som Levemåte.* Samlaget, Oslo.

Griffin, Keith. 1987. *World Hunger and the World Economy.* Macmillan, London.

Gross, J., and S. Rayner. 1985. *Measuring Culture: A Paradigm for the Analysis of Social Organisation.* Columbia University Press, New York.

Gulliver, Philip. 1955. *The Family Herds.* Routledge, London.

Habermas, Jürgen. 1962. *Strukturwandel der Öffentlichkeit.* Luchterhand, Neuwied, Germany.

————. 1973. *Legimitationsprobleme im Spätkapitalismus.* Suhrkamp, Frankfurt am Main, Germany.

————. 1987a. *The Philosophical Discourse of Modernity.* Translated by F. Lawrence. MIT Press, Cambridge, Mass.

————. 1987b. *Theorie des Kommunikativen Handelns Bd. 2 (vierte Auflage).* Suhrkamp, Frankfurt am Main, Germany.

Hacking, Ian. 1983. *Representing and Intervening: Introductory Topics in the Philosophy of Natural Science*. Cambridge University Press, Cambridge, England.

———. 1995. *Rewriting the Soul: Multiple Personality and the Science of Memory*. Princeton University Press, Princeton, N.J.

Hajer, Maarten A. 1993. "Discourse Coalitions and the Institutionalisation of Practice." In Frank Fischer and John Forester, eds., *The Argumentative Turn in Policy Analysis and Planning*, 43–76. Duke University Press, Durham, N.C.

Hazards Forum. 1994. *Risks to the Public: The Rules, the Rulers and the Ruled*. London.

Heclo, Hugh, and Aaron Wildavsky. 1974. *The Private Government of Public Money*. Macmillan, London.

Heelas, D., and A. Locke. 1981. *Indigenous Psychologies: The Anthropology of the Self*. Academic Press, London.

Heimer, Carol. 1985. *Reactive Risk and Rational Action: Managing Moral Hazard in Insurance Contracts*. University of California Press, Berkeley.

Hendriks, Frank. 1994. "Cars and Culture in Munich and Birmingham: The Case for Cultural Pluralism." In Dennis J. Coyle and Richard J. Ellis, eds., *Politics, Policy and Culture*, 51–70. Westview Press, Boulder, Colo.

Hirschman, A. O. 1981. *Shifting Involvements*. Princeton University Press, Princeton, N.J.

Hocart, A. M. 1970 [1936]. *Kings and Councillors: An Essay in the Comparative Anatomy of Human Society*. Edited and with an introduction by Rodney Needham. Classics in Anthropology. University of Chicago Press, Chicago.

Hodgson, Geoffrey M. 1988. *Economics and Institutions: A Manifesto for a Modern Institutional Economics*. Polity Press, Cambridge, England.

———. 1993. "Institutional Economics: Surveying the 'Old' and the 'New.'" *Metreconomica* 44 (1): 1–28.

Hollis, Patricia, ed. 1974. *Pressure from Without in Early Victorian England*. St. Martin's Press, New York.

Hood, Christopher. 1996. "Control over Bureaucracy: Cultural Theory and Institutional Variety." *Journal of Public Policy* 15 (3): 207–230.

Hume, David. 1752. *Political Discourses.* A. Kincaid and A. Donaldson, Edinburgh.

Hunter, Floyd. 1953. *Community Power Structure.* University of North Carolina Press, Chapel Hill.

Inglehart, Ronald. 1990. *Cultural Shift in Advanced Industrial Societies.* Princeton University Press, Princeton, N.J.

Jackson, M., and I. Karp. 1990. *Personhood and Agency: The Experience of Self and Other in African Cultures.* Uppsala Studies in Cultural Anthropology. Acta Universitatis Uppsaliensis, 14. Uppsala, Sweden.

Jacobson-Widding, Anita. 1991. *Body and Space: Symbolic Models of Unity and Division in African Cosmology and Experience.* Uppsala Studies in Cultural Anthropology. Acta Universitatis Uppsaliensis, 16. Uppsala, Sweden.

Jennings, Bruce. 1993. "Counsel and Consensus: Norms of Argument in Health Policy." In Frank Fischer and John Forester, eds., *The Argumentative Turn in Policy Analysis and Planning,* 101–116. Duke University Press, Durham, N.C.

Jevons, William S. 1871. *The Theory of Political Economy.* Macmillan, London.

Kahneman, Daniel, and Amos Tversky. 1981. "The Framing of Decisions and the Psychology of Choice." *Science* 211: 453–458.

———. 1984. "Choices, Values and Frames." *American Psychologist* 39: 341–350.

Kahneman, Daniel, Jack Knetsch, and Richard Thaler. 1986. "Fairness as a Constraint on Profit Seeking: Entitlements in the Market." *American Economic Review* 76 (4): 728–741.

Karmasin, Helene. 1996. *Einstellungen zur Gentechnologie.* Institut für Motivforschung, Vienna.

Katona, George. 1940. *Organising and Memorising: Studies in the Psychology of Learning and Teaching.* Columbia University Press, New York.

———. 1975. *Psychological Economics.* Elsevier, Oxford.

Kelly, George Armstrong. 1992. *The Humane Comedy: Constant, Tocqueville and French Liberalism.* Cambridge University Press, Cambridge, England.

Kierkegaard, S. 1962. *Philosophical Fragments.* Translated by David F. Swenso. Princeton University Press, Princeton, N.J.

Kuhn, T. S. 1977. *The Structure of Scientific Theories.* 2d ed. Edited by Fred Suppes. University of Illinois Press, Urbana.

Lanternari, V. Horio. 1960. *Movimenti religiosi di libertà e di salvezza di popoli oppressi.* Feltrinelli, Milan.

Latour, Bruno. 1988. *Le Microbe: The Pasteurization of France.* Harvard University Press, Cambridge, Mass.

Laufer, Romain. 1993. *L'Entreprise face aux risques majeures.* Harmattan, Paris.

Lederer, Katrin, ed. 1980. *Human Needs: A Contribution to the Current Debate.* Oelgeschlager, Gunn and Hain, Cambridge, Mass.

Leenhardt, Maurice. 1947. *Do Kamo: La Personne et le mythe dans le monde melanésien.* Gallimard, Paris. Reprinted in 1979 as *Do Kamo: Person and Myth in the Melanesian World,* translated by B. M. Gulati, University of Chicago Press, Chicago.

Lewis, David K. 1969. *Convention: A Philosophical Study.* Harvard University Press, Cambridge, Mass.

Lichtenstein, S., P. Slovic, B. Fischhoff, M. Layman, and B. Combs. 1978. "Judged Frequency of Lethal Events." *Journal of Experimental Psychology* 4: 551–578.

Lindblom, C. E. 1965. *The Intelligence of Democracy.* Basic Books, New York.

Luhmann, Niklas. 1984. *Soziale Systeme. Grundriss einer allgemeinen Theorie.* Suhrkamp, Frankfurt am Main, Germany.

Lukes, Stephen. 1974. *Power: A Radical View.* Macmillan, London.

MacLeod, Mary, and Esther Saraga. 1988. "Child Sexual Abuse: Challenging the Orthodoxy." *Feminist Review* 28: 16–55.

Majone, G. 1989. *Evidence, Argument, and Persuasion in the Policy Process.* Yale University Press, New Haven, Conn.

Marris, Claire, Ian Langford, and Timothy O'Riordan. 1996. *Integrating Sociological and Psychological Approaches to Public Perceptions of Environmental Risks: Detailed Results from a Questionnaire Survey.* CSERGE Working Paper GEC 96–07. University of East Anglia, Norwich, England.

Marshall, Alfred. 1920 [1890]. "On Wants and Their Satisfaction." In *The Principles of Economics.* 8th ed., book 3, chap. 6. Macmillan, London.

Marty, Martin E., and Appleby, R. Scott, eds. 1991. *Fundamentalisms Observed.* Vol. 1 of *The Fundamentalism Project.* University of Chicago Press, Chicago.

―――. 1993a. *Fundamentalisms and Society: Reclaiming the Sciences, the Family, and Education.* Vol. 2 of *The Fundamentalism Project.* University of Chicago Press, Chicago.

―――. 1993b. *Fundamentalisms and the State: Remaking Polities, Economies, and Militance.* Vol. 3 of *The Fundamentalism Project.* University of Chicago Press, Chicago.

―――. 1994. *Accounting for Fundamentalisms: The Dynamic Character of Movements.* Vol. 4 of *The Fundamentalism Project.* University of Chicago Press, Chicago.

―――. 1995. *Fundamentalism Comprehended.* Vol. 5 of *The Fundamentalism Project.* University of Chicago Press, Chicago.

Maslow, A. 1943. "A Theory of Human Motivation." *Psychology Review* 50: 370–396.

Maturana, H., and F. Varela. 1980. *Autopoiesis and Cognition: The Realisation of the Living.* Reidl, London.

Mauss, Marcel. 1936. "Les Techniques du corps." *Journal de Psychologie* 32: 3–4. Reprinted in 1950 in *Sociologie et Anthropologie,* 365–386, Presses Universitaires de France, Paris.

―――. 1938. "Une Catégorie de l'esprit humain: La Notion de personne, celle de 'moi'." Reprinted in 1950 in *Sociologie et Anthropologie,* 331–362, Presses Universitaires de France, Paris.

―――. 1950. *Sociologie et anthropologie.* Presses Universitaires de France, Paris.

————. 1979 [1950]. *Seasonal Variations of the Eskimo: A Study in Social Morphology*. Translated by James Fox. Routledge and Kegan Paul, London.

McArthur, Margaret, and Frederick D. McCarthy. 1960. "The Food Quest and the Time-Factor in Aboriginal Economic Life." In C. P. Mountford, ed., *Records of the Australian-American Scientific Expedition to Arnhem Land*, vol. 2, *Anthropology and Nutrition*, 145–194. Melbourne University Press, Melbourne, Australia.

McNeil, William. 1993. "Epilogue, Fundamentalisms and the World of the 1990's." In Martin E. Marty and R. Scott Appleby, eds., *Fundamentalisms and Society: Reclaiming the Sciences, the Family, and Education*, 558–573. Vol. 2 of *The Fundamentalism Project*. University of Chicago Press, Chicago.

Menger, Carl. 1871. *Grundsätze der Volkswirtschaftslehre*. Braumüller, Vienna.

Merton, R. K. 1968. "Social Structure and Anomie." In *Social Theory and Social Science*, enlarged ed., 185–248. Free Press, New York.

Meyer, Aubrey. 1994. *Climate Change, Population and the Paradox of Growth*. Global Commons Institute, London.

Mills, C. W. 1956. *The Power Elite*. Oxford University Press, New York.

Naess, S. 1979. *Om å ha det gedt ibyen og på landet*. Institute of Applied Social Research, Oslo.

Nagel, Thomas. 1986. *The View from Nowhere*. Oxford University Press, Oxford.

Nelson, Richard. 1995. "Recent Evolutionary Theorising about Economic Change." *Journal of Economic Literature* 33: 48–90.

Nelson, Richard, and Sydney Winter. 1982. *An Evolutionary Theory of Economic Change*. Harvard University Press, Cambridge, Mass.

North, Douglass. 1990. *Institutions, Institutional Change and Economic Performance*. Cambridge University Press, Cambridge, England.

Nozick, Robert. 1974. *Anarchy, State, and Utopia*. Basic Books, New York.

Nussbaum, Martha, and Amartya Sen, eds. 1993. *The Quality of Life*. Clarendon Press, Oxford.

Ogien, Albert. 1994. *L'Enquête sur les catégories, de Durkheim à Sacks.* Edited by Bernard Fradin, Louis Quéré, and Jean Widmer, École des Hautes Études en Sciences Sociales, Paris.

Ostrom, Elinor. 1990. *Governing the Commons: The Evolution of Institutions for Collective Action.* Cambridge University Press, Cambridge, England.

Otway, Harry, P. D. Pahner, and J. Linneroth. 1975. *Social Values in Risk Acceptance.* Research Memorandum RM–75–54. IIASA, Laxenburg, Austria.

Parsons, Talcott C. 1937. *The Study of Social Action.* McGraw-Hill, New York.

———. 1939. *The Structure of Social Action.* 2 vols. McGraw-Hill, New York.

———. 1951. *The Social System.* Routledge, London.

———. 1960. "Durkheim's Contribution to the Theory of Social Systems." In Kurt Wolff, *Émile Durkheim, 1858–1917.* Ohio State University Press, Columbus. Shortened and reprinted in 1982 as "Durkheim on Organic Solidarity," in Leon Mayhew, *Talcott Parsons: On Institutions and Social Evolution, Selected Writings,* 189–209, University of Chicago Press, Chicago.

———. 1964. *Essays in Sociological Theory.* Free Press, New York.

Perez-Diaz, V. 1994. *The Challenge of the European Public Sphere.* ASP Paper 4 (c). Complutense University of Madrid, Madrid.

Peterson, M. J. 1992. "Whalers, Cetologists, Environmentalists, and the International Management of Whaling." *International Organisation* 46, no. 1 (Winter): 147–188.

Polsby, Nelson. 1963. *Community Power and Political Theory.* Yale University Press, New Haven, Conn.

———. 1980. *Community Power and Political Theory: A Further Look at Problems of Evidence and Inference.* 2d ed. Yale University Press, New Haven, Conn.

Powell, W., and P. DiMaggio, eds. 1991. *The New Institutionalism in Organizational Analysis.* University of Chicago Press, Chicago.

Putnam, Robert. 1993. *Making Democracy Work: Civic Traditions in Modern Italy*. Princeton University Press, Princeton, N.J.

Raikes, Philip. 1988. *Modernising Hunger: Famine, Food Surplus and Farm Policy in the EEC and Africa*. Catholic Institute of International Relations, London.

Rawls, John. 1971. *A Theory of Justice*. Harvard University Press, Cambridge, Mass.

Rayner, S., and J. Flanagan, eds. 1988. *Rules, Decisions, and Inequality in Egalitarian Societies*. Avebury, Brookfield, Vt.

Rayner, Steve. 1982. "The Perception of Time and Space in Egalitarian Sects: A Millenarian Cosmology." In Mary Douglas, ed., *Essays in the Sociology of Perception*, 247–274. Routledge and Kegan Paul, London.

———. 1988. "The Rules That Keep Us Equal." In J. G. Flanagan and S. Rayner, eds., *Rules, Decisions and Inequality*, 20–42. Avebury, Brookfield, Vt.

———. 1991a. "A Cultural Perspective on the Structure and Implementation of Global Environmental Agreements." *Evaluation Review* 15 (1): 75–102.

———. 1991b. "Expertises et gestion de l'environnement global." In Jacques Theys, ed., *Environnement, science et politique: Les Experts sont formels*. Germes, Paris.

———. 1994. *Governance and the Global Commons*. LSE Centre for Global Governance, Discussion Paper 8. London School of Economics, London.

Renn, O. 1991. "Risk Communication and the Social Amplification of Risk." In R. E. Kasperson and P. J. M. Stallen, eds. *Communicating Risks to the Public*, 287–324. Kluwer, Dordrecht, Netherlands.

Richards, A. I. 1937. *Land, Labour and Diet in Northern Rhodesia*. Oxford University Press, Oxford.

Richards, Paul. 1996a. "Chimpanzees, Diamonds and War: The Discourses of Global Environmental Change and Local Violence on the Liberia–Sierra Leone Border." In Henrietta L. Moore, ed., *The Future of Anthropological Knowledge*, 139–155. Routledge, London.

————. 1996. *Fighting for the Rain Forest: War, Youth and Resources in Sierra Leone.* James Currey for the International African Institute, Oxford.

Riesman, David. 1950. *The Lonely Crowd: A Study of the Changing American Character.* Yale University Press, New Haven, Conn.

Robbins, Lionel. 1952. *The Theory of Economic Policy in English Classical Political Economy.* Macmillan, London.

Roscher, Wilhelm Georg. 1972. *System der Volkswirtschaft.* Translation and reprint of the 1878 ed. published as *Principles of Political Economy,* Arno Press, New York.

Rose-Ackerman, Susan. 1978. *Corruption: A Study in Political Economy.* Academic Press, New York.

The Rowntree Foundation. 1995. *Inquiry as to Income and Wealth.* Vol. 1. Joseph Rowntree Foundation, York, England.

The Royal Society. 1983. *Risk Analysis.* London.

Sahlins, Marshall. 1968. "La Première société d'abondance." *Les Temps Modernes* 268: 641–680. Expanded and reprinted in 1944 as "The Original Affluent Society," in *Stone Age Economics,* Tavistock, London.

————. 1974. *Stone Age Economics,* Tavistock, London.

Samuels, Warren J. 1988. *Institutional Economics.* Edward Elgar, Aldershot, England.

Schelling, Thomas. 1960. *The Strategy of Conflict.* Oxford University Press, New York.

————. 1978. *Micromotives and Macrobehavior.* W. W. Norton, New York.

Schmutzer, Manfred. 1994. *Ingenium und Individium: Eine Sozialwissenschaftliche Theorie von Wissenschaft und Technik.* Springer Verlag, Vienna.

Schwartz, B. I. 1985. *The World of Thought in Ancient China.* Harvard University Press, Cambridge, Mass.

Seckler, D. 1975. *Thorstein Veblen and the Institutionalists: A Study in the Social Philosophy of Economics.* Macmillan, London.

Sen, A. K. 1981. *Poverty and Famines: An Essay on Entitlement and Deprivation.* Clarendon Press, Oxford.

——— . 1985. *Commodities and Capabilities.* North-Holland, Amsterdam.

Shrader-Frechette, K. S. 1991. *Risk and Rationality: Philosophical Foundations for Populist Reforms.* University of California Press, Berkeley.

Simon, Herbert. 1947. *Administrative Behavior.* Macmillan, New York.

Sivan, Emmanuel. 1995. "The Enclave Culture." In Martin E. Marty and R. Scott Appleby, eds., *Fundamentalism Comprehended,* 11–68. Vol. 5 of *The Fundamentalism Project.* University of Chicago Press, Chicago.

Slovic, Paul. 1992. "Perceptions of Risk: Reflections on the Psychometric Paradigm." In S. Krimsky and D. Golding, eds., *Social Theories of Risk,* 117–152. Praeger, Westport, Conn.

Spencer, Herbert. 1876. *The Principles of Sociology.* Williams and Norgate, London.

Starr, Chauncy. 1969. "Social Benefit versus Technological Risk." *Science,* 1232–1238.

Strathern, Marilyn. 1988. *The Gender of the Gift: Problems with Women and Problems with Society in Melanesia.* University of California Press, Berkeley.

——— . 1992. *Reproducing the Future: Essays on Anthropology, Kinship and the New Reproductive Technologies.* Routledge, New York.

Swedlow, Brendan. 1994. "Cultural Influences on Policies concerning Mental Health." In Dennis J. Coyle and Richard J. Ellis, eds., *Politics, Policy and Culture,* 71–89. Westview Press, Boulder, Colo.

Taylor, Michael. 1982. *Community, Anarchy and Liberty.* Cambridge University Press, Cambridge, England.

Thévenot, Laurent. 1995. "L'Action publique contre l'exclusion dans des approches pluralistes du juste." In Joelle Affichard and Jean-Baptiste de Foucauld, eds., *Pluralisme et équité: La Justice sociale dans les democraties,* 41–70. Editions Esprit, Paris.

Thompson, M., and M. Schwarz. 1990. *Divided We Stand: Redefining Politics, Technology and Social Choice.* Wheatsheaf, Brighton, England.

Thompson, Michael. 1979. *Rubbish Theory: The Creation and Destruction of Value.* Oxford University Press, Oxford.

Turnbull, Colin. 1961. *The Forest People.* Simon and Schuster, New York.

———. 1964. *Wayward Servants: The Two Worlds of the African Pygmies.* Eyre and Spottiswode, London.

Turner, Brian. 1991. Preface to the 1991 edition of Talcott Parsons, *The Social System*, xviii–xlv. Routledge, London.

UNDP [United Nations Development Programme]. 1990. *Human Development Report, 1990.* Oxford University Press, Oxford and New York.

———. 1991. *Human Development Report, 1991.* Oxford University Press, New York.

Varian, Hal R. 1974. "Equity, Envy and Efficiency." *Journal of Economic Theory* 9: 63–91.

Wagner, P., B. Wittrock, and R. Whitley. 1991. *Discourses on Society: The Shaping of the Social Science Disciplines.* Kluwer Academic Publishers, Dordrecht, Netherlands.

Wagner, P., C. Hirschon Weiss, B. Wittrock, and H. Wollman, 1991. *Social Sciences and Modern States: National Experiences and Theoretical Crossroads.* Cambridge University Press, Cambridge, England.

Wagner, Peter. 1991. "Science of Society Lost: On the Failure to Establish Sociology in Europe during the Classical Period." In P. Wagner, B. Wittrock, R. Whitley, eds., *Discourses on Society: The Shaping of the Social Science Disciplines*, 219–245. Kluwer Academic Publishers, Dordrecht, Netherlands.

Walras, Léon. 1874. *Éléments d'économie politique pure: ou Théorie de la richesse sociale.* Corbaz, Lausanne, Switzerland.

Walzer, Michael. 1995. "Exclusion, injustice et état démocratique." In Joelle Affichard and Jean-Baptiste de Foucauld, eds., *Pluralisme et équité: La Justice sociale dans les democraties*, 29–40. Editions Esprit, Paris.

Warner, Frederick. 1992. "Calculated Risks." *Science and Public Affairs* Winter: 44–49.

Weber, Max. 1949. "The Logic of the Cultural Sciences." In *Max Weber on the Methodology of the Social Sciences*. Free Press, New York.

Whistler, James McNeil. 1967 [1840]. *The Gentle Art of Making Enemies*. Dover Publications, New York.

Wildavsky, A. 1975. *Budgeting: A Comparative Theory of Budgetary Processes*. Little, Brown, Boston.

———. 1980. *How to Limit Government Spending*. University of California Press, Berkeley.

Wilder, Thornton. 1973. *Theophilus North*. Harper and Row, New York.

Williamson, Oliver E. 1975. *Hierarchies and Markets: Analysis and Anti-Trust Implications*. Collier Macmillan, London.

Wittgenstein, L. 1953. *Philosophical Investigations*. Blackwell, Oxford.

Woodburn, James. 1968. "Introduction to Hadza Ecology." In Richard B. Lee and Irven DeVore, eds., *Man the Hunter*, 49–55. Aldine, Chicago.

Wynne, B. 1982. *Rationality and Ritual: The Windscale Enquiry and Nuclear Decisions in Britain*. British Society for the History of Science, Chalfont St. Giles, England.

———. 1992. "Risk and Social Learning." In S. Krimsky and D. Golding, eds., *Social Theories of Risk*, 275–297. Praeger, New York.

INDEX

Abensour, Miguel, 4

Access. *See* Public policy process

Accountability: global dispersal of, 181; peer group, 178, 180

Acid-rain discourse, 126–127

Ackerman, Bruce, 97

Ad hominem arguments, 85

Affluence: constituent elements of, 2–3; and political freedom, 3–4; in primitive cultures, 3

Africa, 59, 63, 65

Alienation, 148, 160, 161

Allardt, E., 51

Allocation, social mechanisms of, 71–72; and famine, 58–61

Altruism: and hierarchy of values, 48–49; and industrialization, 2; non-Western concepts of, 9, 93; and standard of living, 49

Ambiguity, 178; of authority

within sects, 149, 150–152; versus social constructs, 126; tolerance of, 15

Analogies: in physical nature, 34–35; physiological, 38–43; scientific, 28–29

Anomie or normlessness, 159

Anthropology, 166–167; and bread-in-the-belly theory, 48–49; and defining humans as nonsocial, 8–9; and folk psychology, 82–83

Anthropomorphization: of market theory, 39–40, 43. *See also* Economic man

Anti-institutionalist bias. *See* Institutions

Appleby, R. Scott, 142–144

Archeology, 158

Ardener, Shirley, 84

Argumentation processes, 125–
126; cultural basis of, 126–128
Art, the need for, 47, 48
Arthur, Brian, 170
Atrocities, and cultural bias, 117,
119–120
Attitudes: cultural audits of,
139–140, 140n1; toward well-
being, 122–123
Audits, peer-group, 178, 180
Authority, global dispersal of, 181
Automobile engines, 170
Autopoiësis, 31
Avoidance of alignment. *See* Iso-
lates, the culture of
Ayres, Clarence, 158

Background conditions, the idea
of, 71–72
Balance sheets, progress and dep-
rivation, 64, 65–68
Basic-needs discourse, 5–7
Beck, Ulrich, 136
Bernouilli, Daniel, 33–34, 43
Berreman, Gerald D., 4
Bias, cultural. *See* Cultural bias;
Cultural types, the four
Birmingham road planning, 133
Boltanski, Luc, 21, 97, 99, 100, 182
Book, the Sacred, 150–151
Boulding, Kenneth, 20, 163
Bourdieu, Pierre, 17–18, 19–20
Bread-in-the-belly theory, 47–49
Britain, public discourse in,
126–127
British civil service, 179
Brunner, Christian, 104, 105 (fig.),
141, 142 (fig.)
Buchanan, James, 158
Budget, household, 182; Engel's
law of, 42–43

Bureaucracy: and democracy,
134; as hierarchical, 104–105
(fig.), 151, 173, 176–177, 179–
180
Bureaucrats, 104–105 (fig.)
Burke, Kenneth, 84

Caillé, Alain, 20
Canaque persons, 11–13
Capital, social, 69, 72, 130
Capitalism: and institutions, 158;
and loss of civic input, 115–116;
and pluralism, 121
Censorship: and control of knowledge, 148–149, 150–151, 181,
183
Centering. *See* Microcosmic thinking
Centralization, and hierarchy,
182–183
Certainties, contradictory, 104
Chancism form of public administration, 178
Change: industrial-world social,
68; institutional, 169–173; personal choice and social, 92–95;
technological, 170–171,
180–183
Children: education and cultural
contexts of, 108; health and
mortality of, 65; persons as feral,
79–80, 90–91; in sects, 148–
149
Choice: disregarding cultural
influence on, 77, 79; economic
man and rational, 44–45, 78–
79; among household cultures,
109–112, 111 (fig.); influences
on human development, 63;
whole persons as having, 92–
95, 173, 184. *See also* Public

policy process, the; Rational choice
Choicism form of public administration, 179
Christianity, 152; and rationality, 75, 155
Cities, parables and fictions comparing, 97–100
City roads, planning, 133
Civic responsiveness, 130–134; measures of, 132–133
Civic world, the, 97
Civil liberties, 69–72, 157
Civil service, British, 179
Civil wars, intransigence of, 119–120
Classical economics, 155–156, 172
Clifford, James, 11, 12
Closure. *See* Enclave culture
Coalitions. *See* Discourse coalitions; Public policy process, the
Coase, Ronald, 165
Cognitive psychology: nonhuman, 86–88; and universal logic, 77–80, 175
Coleman, James, 161
Collectivity: and cultural bias, 102
Collegiality, 178
Collingridge, David, 129
Commercial world, the, 97
Commons, John, 158
Communication: through tastes, 53–58, 55 (fig.), 57 (fig.); technology, 68, 73, 182–183
Communication needs: and civic responsiveness, 130–134; of social beings, 46–47, 72–73
Communism, 132, 142, 147, 161
Community, closed. *See* Enclave culture

Comparisons. *See* International comparisons; Social sciences
Competition: between cultural types, 100–101, 103, 104–106; education for, 108; and individualism, 179, 182; public administration control by, 179
Compromise, 141; and consensus, 129, 152; as unthinkable, 150
Computer literacy, 72–73
Conflicts of interest: individual versus community, 76, 114; in the public sphere, 128–130
Conscience. *See* Enclave culture; Morality
Consensus, 129, 152
Conspiracy theory, bias toward, 102, 146, 148
Constant, Benjamin, 157
Constitutional preferences, 91–92
Construction, social, 121–122
Consumer behavior: background conditions of life and, 69–72; constraints on, 41–42; physiological model of, 39–40, 43; and tastes, 53–58, 55 (fig.), 57 (fig.)
Consumption theory, 7; and altruism, 9; and Engel's Law, 42–43; and living as a production process, 69–72; prices and income in, 37–38; problems with physiological basis of, 40–43; and social relationships, 53–58
Contracts, choice of, 166
Contradictions, thought, 104, 167
Control of knowledge: by enclave culture, 148–149, 150–151, 181, 183; by hierarchy, 182–183
Control strategies: in public management, 176–180; technologies and institutional, 180–183

Controversies: enclavism and increase in, 140–141; intransigent, 119–120, 129–130, 133–134, 149–150; as risk debates, 135–136, 140–141; show of emotions in, 141, 142 (fig.)

Conventions, study of, 171–172

Cooperation: and civic responsiveness, 130–134; and groupism, 178–179; and smallness of scale, 167–169. *See also* Discourse coalitions

Coordination problems, 171

Corruption, and bureaucracy, 178

Coser, Lewis, 146

Cost-benefit strategies, 87–88, 124

Cultural bias: challenges in classifying, 99–100, 107–108; against institutions, 157–162, 179, 182, 184; ignoring or confronting, 174–176; as inherently adversarial, 104–106, 122–123, 125, 141, 142 (fig.), 153; parables and fictions of, 97–99; in psychology, 51–52; in sociology, 161–162

Cultural needs, theories of basic, 49–52

Cultural theory: on enclave development, 147–149, 172–173; and institutional variety, 176–180; and personal choice, 92–95, 173, 184; and rational persons, 184; and relative wealth, 100, 112; and saying nothing, 175–176

Cultural types, the four: in adversarial democracy, 104–106, 122–123, 141, 153; civic responsiveness to all, 130–131; cultural audits of allegiance to, 139–140,

140n1; cultural map of, 101 (fig.), 102–103; as discourse coalitions, 126–128; dominance factors, 180–183; of households, 109–112, 111 (fig.); and intransigence, 117–120, 129–130; labeling of, 103; as a parsimonious model, 100–101; within persons, 93, 106–109, 109 (fig.); as plural rationalities, 104; public policy ideas of, 122–125; and risk perception, 136–138; and technological conditions, 180–183; weaknesses of, 181–183. *See also* Institutions; Person, theory of the whole

Cultural-argument system, the, 125–128

Cumulative technology theory, 170

Curiosity, reasons for lack of, 94

Cybernetic society, 163

Dahl, Robert A., 121

Dake, Karl, 110–111, 139

Danger. *See* Risk perception

Darwin, Charles, 28

Dasgupta, Partha, 69–70

Dawkins, Richard, 25–26

Decision making. *See* Egalitarianism; Public policy process, the; Rationality

Deductivism, formal, 155, 172

Defection, preventing, 148–149

Demand and prices, 34

Democracy: four-sided cultural conflict in, 104–106; four types of, 177–180; fundamentalism as adversarial to, 142–143, 144; genuine pluralism in, 125, 134; the isolates in, 115–116; and pluralism, 15, 131; protection of ideals of, 17. *See also* Public policy process, the

Dennett, Daniel C., 13, 26–27, 90–91, 94

Depression and prosperity, cultural audit of, 138–139

Deprivation: fundamentalism as caused by, 144–145; index of human, 63–64

Destitution, 5, 7

Developing countries: famines in, 59; human-deprivation index indicators in, 64, 65–66

Deviance: from rationality, 80–84; sectarianism as form of, 144

Deviants, expulsion of, 146, 179

Dialogue: and civic responsiveness, 130–134; the cultural-argument system of, 125–128; and justification, 21, 122–125; and public conflict, 128–130

Diminishing marginal satisfaction theory, 33–36

Diplomacy, 117–118, 151–152

Disappointment, 82, 95

Discourse coalitions: acid-rain debate between, 126–127; enclave avoidance of, 146–147, 148, 149–150

Disintegration, social, 119–120; and institutions, 158–159, 159–160

"Disorganized bureaucracy," 178

Dissent, evolution toward total, 147–149, 172. *See also* Enclave culture

Distress, 84–86

Distribution: of communication technology, 73, 181, 182–183; of goods, 53–54; of income, 64, 65, 67

Domestic world, the, 97

Douglas, Mary, 7, 53, 73, 89, 114, 122, 149, 169, 175

Drewnowski, J., 49–50

Driving side of the road, 171

Du Maurier, George, 54, 55 (fig.), 56

Duclos, Denis, 136

Dunbar, R. I. M., 80, 87, 90

Durkheim, Émile, 11, 13–14, 20, 21, 46, 159

Ecomodernists and pragmatists, 126

Econometry, 7

Economic man: egoist principles of, 44, 46; in market theory, 37–38; as pervasive microcosm, 22–23, 33, 44–45; physiology of, 39–43; responsibility for theory of, 43–44; saying nothing about, 175–176; as a signal, 41; tool-to-theory heuristic of, 33, 74; as unculturated, 51–52; in utility theory, 38–40. *See also* Person, social sciences and the; Persons, rational

Economic theory: American, 158; classical, 155–156, 172; English, 157–158; French, 157; German, 155; and measurability, 5, 6–7, 8, 17, 132–133, 165; neoclassical, 164–165; New Institutionalism in, 163–166; and poverty theory, 5; responsibility for changing, 44; and theory of institutions, 154–157, 163–166; and utility theory, 36–38. *See also* Market theory; Utility theory

Education: cultural-bias contexts of, 108; indicators, 50, 65, 67; sectarian, 148–149, 150–151

Efficiency, concepts of, 76, 168

Egalitarianism, 149–150; and decision making, 150–152. *See also* Enclave culture

Egoist principles: of economic man, 44, 46, 61; four types of, 106–109, 109 (fig.)

Éléments d'économie politique pure: ou Théorie de la richesse sociale (Walras), 34

Ellis, Richard, 101–102, 104, 115, 138

Elster, Jon, 82

Emotions: and cultural bias, 117–120, 134; as deviant from rational norm, 80–84; doing service for explanation, 84–86, 94, 144–145, 147, 168; and risk perception, 84–85. *See also* Controversies

Employer-employee losses and gains, 7–79

Employment: administrative controls of, 177–180; and income indicators, 67

Empowerment, political, 150–152

Enclave culture: and communication technology, 181; conspiracy fears of, 102, 146, 148; control of knowledge by the, 148–149, 150–151, 181, 183; on the cultural map, 101 (fig.), 102; decision making, 150–152; defection from, 148–149; the development of, 147–149; of dissenting movements, 85–86, 118, 146–147; ecomodernists as an, 126–127; as egalitarian, 146, 149; exclusivity of, 145–147, 148; factiousness of, 103–104, 145, 150, 181; versus hierarchy, 117–120, 126–127, 133–134, 137–138; the holy man of, 104–105 (fig.); versus individualism, 128, 133; institutional organization of, 118–119, 185; leadership authority in, 151–152; and mental-health policy, 127; and mutuality, 178–179; policy process bias of, 123; possibility of, 185; problems of, 145–150; and risk perception, 137–138, 139, 140–141; strengths of, 181; the three pillars of, 148–149; weaknesses of the, 102, 118–119, 181; and wealth, 52, 148; and zealotry, 152–153, 185

Ends and means, 76

Engel, Ernst, 42

Engel's Law, 42–43

Engines, gas, 170

Enmity, 119–120, 153

Entitlements, and infrastructures, 58–61

Environmentalism, 56; cultural bias and, 123–124, 126–127, 130; and risk perception, 137–140

Environments, social: concept of enabling, 71–72; progress and deprivation in, 66, 68. *See also* Cultural types, the four

Envy, choices ascribed to, 81, 83, 94

Equality, political, 3–4. *See also* Public policy process, the

Equilibria, models of, 33–34, 36–37

Erikson, R., 49, 51, 52

Ethnomethodology, 84
Evans-Pritchard, E. E., 84
Evolution: institutional, 172–173;
    technological, 170, 171
Evolutionism: new, 163–165, 170;
    and random events, 170; social,
    157, 167
Exclusion: by disparagement, 84;
    from policy processes, 115–116,
    182; from wealth, 116
Exclusivity, of enclave culture,
    145–147
Extremism, political, 116, 147; and
    violence, 119–120

Factionalism. *See* Enclave culture
Family, the, 68; as hierarchy, 182;
    varied household cultures of,
    109–112, 111 (fig.)
Famine: and inadequate infrastruc-
    tures, 58–61; statistics, 68
Fatalism, bias toward, 102, 114,
    137, 178
Fate, and innovation, 170, 171
Fear and dread, 81–82, 141
Feedback cycle, cultural, 31,
    91–92, 93, 123–124, 163
Feral child, person as, 79–80,
    90–91
Fischer, Frank, 125
Flanagan, J., 102
Folk psychology, 82–83
Food analogy, utility theory, 34–35
"Food availability decline" (FAD),
    59–60
Forester, John, 125
Foucault, M., 84, 95
Four cultural types. *See* Cultural
    types, the four
Freedom: and affluence, 3–4; and
    civic responsiveness, 130–134;

and civil liberties, 69–72, 157; of
    isolates, 103; political, 63, 69,
    125, 184; positive and negative,
    69, 71, 72; without technology,
    2–3, 167–169
"Fruit machine" model of bureau-
    cracy, 178
Frustration, choices ascribed to,
    82, 94, 95, 144–145
Functionalist sociology, 160
Fundamentalism: deprivation as
    cause of, 144–145; and renewal,
    118–119; studying religious,
    142–145. *See also* Enclave cul-
    ture
Fundamentalism Project, 142–
    144

Galtung, Johan, 7
Gasper, Des, 7
Genestier, Philippe, 17–18, 19–20
Genetic theory, 25, 26
George, Vic, 2
Gifts, persons as, 9, 93
Gigerenzer, Gerd, 30–31, 36
Global climate change (GCC)
    controversy, 123–124, 133–134
Globalization: and accountability,
    181; and good taste, 56, 58; and
    social theories, 15–16, 19
Glove, problem of the, 13
God, as focusing agent, 135
Goffman, Erving, 161
Goldstein, D., 30–31
Good. *See* Morality
Good taste, 53–58, 55 (fig.), 57
    (fig.)
Goodman, David, 2
Goods. *See* Things and goods
Goody, Esther, 86
Gould, Stephen Jay, 28

Gouldner, Alvin, 160
Greed: institutional, 146; and utility theory, 35
Greens, sectarian, 124, 133
Grendstad, Gunnar, 140n1
Griffin, Keith, 2
Gross domestic product (GDP), 63
Gross national product (GNP), 66, 67
Groupism, control by, 178–179
Groups, the four cultural. See Cultural types, the four
Gulliver, Philip, 3

Habermas, Jürgen, 115–116
Hajer, Maarten A., 126
HDI (United Nations Human Development Index), 61, 62–69
Health: indicators, 50, 65, 66; mental, 127–128
Heclo, Hugh, 179
Heelas, D., 83
Heimer, Carol, 169
Hendriks, Frank, 133
Hierarchies: of expenditure, 42; of needs, 39–40, 47–48; of values, 47–48
Hierarchy, the culture of: bias against, 157–162, 179, 182; as bureaucratic, 104–105 (fig.), 151, 173, 176–177, 179–180; and communication technology, 182–183; versus competitive individualism, 114, 128, 133–134; and control of knowledge, 182–183; on the cultural map, 101 (fig.), 102; cultures based on, 52, 79; versus enclavists, 117–120, 126–127, 133, 137–138, 152; and mental-

health policy, 127; policy process bias of, 122–123; pragmatist voice of, 126–127; and risk perception, 137–138, 139–140. See also Institutions
Higher needs, theories of, 49–52. See also Needs; Wants
Hirschman, A. O., 82
Historical School economics, 155–156
Histories: reconstructing national, 16–17; typical enclave, 147–150
History of ideas: and analogies, 28–29, 34–35, 38–43; and memes, 25–29, 34–35; and metaphors, 28–29; and social practice, 29, 96. See also Microcosmic thinking; specific science or theory names
Hocart, A. M., 24, 26, 28
Hodgson, Geoffrey M., 44, 163–164
Hollis, Patricia, 147
Homo œconomicus. See Economic man
Hood, Christopher, 177–180
Households: the culture of, 109–112, 111 (fig.); income and expenditure of, 42–43
Human body analogies, 34–35, 39–40
Human development: the concept of, 63; contexts and psychology of, 106–109. See also Education
Human Development Index (HDI), 61, 62–69. See also Primitive cultures
Human needs. See Needs, human
Human rights. See Rights
Human-deprivation Index, the HDI, 63–64, 65–68

Hume, David, 33
Hunger: analogies of desire and, 39; and bread-in-the-belly theory, 47–49; world, 65, 68
Hunting and gathering societies, 3–4

Idea of cultural types. *See* Cultural types, the four
Ideas of the person. *See* Person, social sciences and the
Ignorance, cultivating, 94, 175–176
Income, 7; and household expenditure, 42–43; indicators and, 64, 65, 67; national, 62–63, 64, 65–68; surplus, 50, 51; and welfare indicators, 50. *See also* Standard of living
Indian subcontinent famines, 59
Individualism, the culture of, 79; and competition, 179, 182; on the cultural map, 101 (fig.), 102; versus enclavists, 133, 153; versus hierarchy, 114, 127–128, 133–134; and involuntary isolates, 182; and markets, 114, 129; and mental-health policy, 127; of pioneers, 104–105 (fig.); and pluralism, 121–122, 131; policy process bias of, 122; and rational man, 103, 122; and risk perception, 137, 139; weaknesses of, 181–182. *See also* Choice
Individuals: institutional control of, 157–162; well-being of institutions or, 69–70
Industrial world, the, 2, 97, 182; human-deprivation index of, 63, 66–68. *See also* Environmentalism; Technologies
Information costs, 165, 168

Information system, society as a, 163
Infrastructure roads, 133
Infrastructures, social: of communication, 72–73; entitlements approach to, 58–61; international comparisons of, 61–69, 72
Inglehart, Ronald, 49
Injustice. *See* Justice
"Inner quality of life," components of, 52
Innovation, technological, 170, 171, 180
Institution, as pejorative term, 159, 182
Institutionalism: historical, 154–157, 164; New, 163–166, 176
Institutionalization, 161; and mental health, 127–128
Institutions: bias against, 157–162, 179, 182, 184; cultural map of four types of, 101 (fig.); as culture-bearing, 174; economic development support by, 168–169; economic science and study of, 154–157, 162; four strategies of control in, 176–180; ideas as embedded in, 6; incentives to design, 164; individuals subordinate to well-being of, 69–70; and moral purposes, 159–160, 164–165, 174; in New Institutionalism, 163–166; as of one type, 162, 177; and the prevailing technology, 180–183; protection offered by, 169; self-perpetuation of, 177; as shackling individuals, 157–162; the technological base of, 180–183. *See also* Cultural types, the four; Religions

Intelligence, nonhuman, 86–88
Intentional systems, persons as, 90–91; with social intentions, 91–93
International comparisons, 72; human-deprivation index, 63–64; the person in, 61–69; of religious enclaves, 150–151
International studies: of bias and risk, 140n1; of religious fundamentalism, 142–145
Interpretation of knowledge, sectarian, 148–149, 150–151
Irreconcilable disagreement, 129–130
Isherwood, Baron, 73
Isolates, the culture of, 113–116; in adversarial democracy, 104, 115–116; and communication technology, 182; and contrived randomness, 177–178; on the cultural map, 101 (fig.), 102; the effect of individualism on, 182; fatalism in, 102, 114, 137, 178; freedom in, 103; policy process bias of, 123; and risk perception, 137
Italy, regional politics in, 131–132

Jackson, M., 14
Jacobson-Widding, Anita, 14
Jealousy, the microcosm as, 24–25, 76
Jevons, William S., 34
Justice: and civic responsiveness, 130–134; and cultural conflict, 119–120, 134; and emotions, 94; and ideas of fairness, 52, 78–79, 149; injustice and failures of, 119–120, 134; insults to ideas of, 119–120, 134; measures of, 62,

73; of one god, 135; plural doctrines of, 97–98, 117–119; and punishment, 108, 168; risk and talking about, 135–136; and social responsibilities, 70, 81
Justification of persons theory, 97–98; and cultural bias theory, 113

Kahneman, Daniel, 77–78
Kant, Immanuel, 20
Karmasin, Helene, 140n1
Karp, I., 14
Katona, George, 41
Keynes, John Maynard, 37–38
Kings and Councillors: An Essay in the Comparative Anatomy of Human Society (Hocart), 24, 26, 28
Kinship, economy embedded in, 169
Knowledge: control of, 148–149, 150–151, 181, 182–183; nomological, 89; nonhuman, 86–88
Kuhn, T. S., 30

Lack, poverty as, 5
Land, diminishing returns from, 33, 34, 35, 43
Langford, Ian, 140n1
Language: and bias, 103, 140n1, 182; of cultural conflict, 119–120, 124; formalism of economics, 156, 184; about institutions, 159, 182
Lanternari, V. Horio, 86
Latour, Bruno, 28–29
Laufer, Romain, 136
Le Play, Frédéric, 42n1
Leadership: enclave, 149–152
Leenhardt, Maurice, 11–13

Leiris, Michael, 12
Leisure and recreation, 3, 50
Level of Living Index (Drewnow-
ski and Scott), 49–51
Liberalism: influence of, 121–122,
131, 155; religious fundamental-
ism as adversarial to, 143, 144,
152; and rising living standards,
49. *See also* Individualism, the
culture of
Life expectancy, 63, 64; and
health, 65, 66
Lindblom, C. E., 128
Lions, listening to, 12–13
Literacy rates, 63, 64, 65
Litmus test for cultural bias, 140
Locke, A., 83
Loneliness, 84–86; and anomie,
159
Losses and gains, principle of
asymmetrical, 77–79
Lottery, decision making by, 151
Luhmann, Niklas, 123

McArthur, Margaret, 3
McCarthy, Frederick D., 3
McNeil, William, 118–119,
144–145
Macrocosm and microcosm, 24–25
Male gender of *homo œconomicus*,
23
Malthus, Thomas Robert, 5, 48
Map, the four-part cultural, 101
(fig.), 102–103; and four ego
types, 109 (fig.); and four house-
hold cultures, 110, 111 (fig.),
112
Marginal propensity to consume,
37–38, 43
Marginalist revolution, 34
Marginality, 157; and capitalism,

115–116; folk psychology effect
on, 84. *See also* Deviance
Margins, substitution at the,
165–166
Market theory, 36–37, 156;
anthropomorphization of,
38–40; and public policy con-
flict, 128–130; social evolution-
ist, 157, 167; and wants, 42–43,
44, 95. *See also* Economic theory
Marris, Claire, 140n1
Marshall, Alfred, 35, 43
Marty, Martin E., 142–144
Marx, Karl, 5
Marxism, 155, 157
Maslow, A., 47, 49
Mass unemployment, 37
Mauss, Marcel, 10–11, 13–14
Medical care, 65, 127–128
Melanesian persons, 9, 93
Membership in sects, 148–149
Memes, 25–29; based on physical
nature, 34–35; definition and
characteristics of, 26; success of,
27–28
Men: disaffected young, 116; as
homo œconomicus, 23
Menger, Carl, 34
Mental-health policy, 127–128
Merit: peer review of, 178, 180;
plural judgments of, 98–99
Metaphors, success of, 28–29
Meyer, Aubrey, 124
Microcosm: the clock, 30, 36; as
group-think, 43; the jealous,
24–25, 76; the king's body, 24,
32; the rational-choice, 121
Microcosmic levels of utility theory, 39–40, 182–183
Microcosmic thinking, 23, 184;
cultural theory of four-part,

Microcosmic thinking (*continued*)
105–106; institutionalization of,
36–38; as a meme, 27–29,
31–32, 39–40; replication and
reinforcement of, 36–38; risk as
bridging concept in, 135–136;
tools as inspiring, 29–33; as universal, 24, 25
Microeconomic studies, 172, 176
Middle-class fundamentalism, 145
Mind, building a social model of,
90–92
Minorities: exclusivity of, 148; theories on dissenting, 85–86, 118,
146–147. *See also* Enclave culture
Missing persons: reinstallation of,
174, 184–185; the three politically active, 104–105 (fig.). *See
also* Cultural types, the four
Montesquieu, Charles de Secon-
dat, 3
Morality: and choice, 184; and
conscience, 46; education
emphasizing, 108, 150–151; and
institutional purposes, 159–160,
164–165, 174; and taste, 56–58,
57 (fig.)
Mortality, 50, 65, 66
Multinational corporations, 181
Munich road planning, 133
Mutuality form of public administration, 178–179
Mythic participations, 11–14

Naess, S., 52
Nagel, Thomas, 19
National identities, myths of,
16–17
Nations, entitlements approach to
studying, 58–61

Nature: analogies from, 34–35, 38–
43; poverty blamed on, 59–60
Needham, Rodney, 25
Needs, human: abstract, 6–7; basic
cultural, 49–52; communication, 46–47, 72–73, 130–134,
181–183; entitlements approach
to, 58–61; four levels of, 5–7;
having, loving, and being, 51;
hierarchies of, 39–40; lower and
higher, 6–7, 47–52; materialist
and postmaterialist, 49; symbolic
and instrumental, 47; and tastes,
53–58, 55 (fig.), 57 (fig.); theories of two types of, 46–47. *See
also* Higher needs; Wants
Negative freedom, 69–70
Negotiation: and compromise,
129, 141, 150, 152; and empowerment, 150–152
Nelson, Richard, 164, 170–171
Networks: kinship, 169; and sects,
146–147
Neutralization, of political bias,
175–176
New Caledonian Canaque, 11–13
New Institutionalism, 163–166,
176
Newport, the nine cities of, 98–99;
reclassifying, 112–113
Nondiscrimination within sects,
149
Nonhuman intelligence studies,
86–88
Normlessness or anomie, 159
Norms: civic virtues or, 130–131;
institutional, 156, 159; of ration-
ality, 80–84
North, Douglass, 167
Nothing, preferring to say, 10,
174, 175–176

Novy, Pat, 57 (fig.), 109 (fig.)
Nozick, Robert, 81
Nuclear technology, 129–130, 140
Number of worlds or cultural
    biases, selecting the, 100–102
Numeracy, 72
Nussbaum, Martha, 52
Nutrition indicators, 50, 64, 68

Objectivity: demanding total,
    17–20; foregrounding, 124; and
    generality to avoid politics, 76,
    89, 94, 129; of human needs the-
    ories, 51–52; the ideal of, 14,
    17–20, 95; of saying nothing, 10,
    175–176; and typification, 107.
    See also Rationality
Onion-skin image of the person,
    80, 90–91
Opinion, the world of, 97
Opportunity costs, 78–79
Organizations. *See* Institutions
O'Riordan, Timothy, 140n1
Outrage, and cultural bias,
    117–120, 134

Parsons, Talcott C., 156, 159, 161
Pasteur, Louis, 28–29
Path dependency, 170, 171, 176
Path of least resistance, 27,
    172–173, 176
Patients, care of mental-health,
    127–128
Peace: conferences, 117–118; and
    cultural bias, 119–120, 152
Peer groups, accountability in,
    178, 180. *See also* Enclave cul-
    ture
Perez-Diaz, Victor, 16–17
Person, social sciences and the: as
    decentered, 11–12; as duplex,

46–47; and empathy, 84–86; and
    folk psychology, 83–84; and
    institutions, 154, 160–161; and
    justification, 20–21; as locus of
    transactions, 8–11, 91–92,
    93–94; as materialist and post-
    materialist, 49; in New Institu-
    tionalism, 164–166; and nonhu-
    man intelligence studies, 86–88;
    as nonrelational, 9, 10, 129, 184;
    as other-directed, 9, 177–179; as
    political, 14, 164, 185; and
    rationality, 75–77, 129, 164; and
    risk, 136; as role-playing and
    self-aware, 10–11; as the same
    everywhere, 51–52, 129; as a
    taboo area, 88–89; and universal
    emotions, 80–86, 94; and uni-
    versal logic, 77–80. *See also*
    Social sciences
Person, theories of the: disinterest
    in alternate, 10; need for, 88–89,
    96–97, 185; problems in revis-
    ing, 13–14, 20–21; in Western
    civilization, 10–11. *See also spe-
    cific science or theory names*
Person, theory of the whole: and
    bounded rationality, 120–122;
    and cultural feedback, 91–93;
    and four types of ego, 106–109;
    and having political and moral
    choice, 92–95, 173, 184–185; as
    an intentional system, 90–91,
    91–93; need for articulating a,
    88–89, 96–97, 185; problems
    without a, 74–95; in the public
    process, 129–130; qualities nec-
    essary for a, 89; as social, 89–90,
    100–104, 185. *See also* Cultural
    types, the four
Personal choice. *See* Choice

Personality types and ego in four, 106–109, 139–140

Personnage, the concept of, 10–11

Persons: basic cultural needs of, 49–52; cultural types within, 93, 106–109, 109 (fig.); as feral children, 79–80, 90–91; in international comparisons, 61–69; needs of nonsocial, 5–7, 8. *See also* Person, theories of the

Persons, rational: four kinds of, 174; needs of aggregated individual, 51–52. *See also* Economic man

Persons (the term), or *people*, 184

Peterson, M. J., 130

Pioneers, 104–105 (fig.)

Plural rationalities. *See* Cultural types, the four

Pluralism, politics of, 15, 94, 96, 185; foregrounding the, 124; genuine, 125, 133; individualist bias of, 131; and legitimacy, 150–151; marketplace analogy to, 128–129; and policy analysis, 121–122, 133, 138–141. *See also* Politics

Polarization, 132, 140n1

Policy analysis: and cultural audits, 138–141; and pluralism, 121, 133, 138–141

Policy conflicts, 185; cultural audits of, 138–141; depolarization of, 132; intransigent, 128–130, 149–150

Policy sciences: analysis of argumentation, 125–126; and bounded rationality, 120–122

Political action. *See* Public policy process

Political correctness, and taste, 56–58, 57 (fig.)

Political freedom. *See* Freedom

Politicization. *See* Enclave culture

Politics: and civic responsiveness, 130–134; and extremism, 116; neutralization of, 175–176; risk debates as, 141; three missing persons in, 104–105 (fig.); using objectivity to avoid, 76, 89, 94, 137; and violence, 119–120. *See also* Objectivity; Pluralism, politics of

Polsby, Nelson, 121

Poor persons, 65, 67; people problems of, 20; survey of, 17–19. *See also* Human Development Index (HDI); Primitive cultures

Population progress and deprivation, 68

Positive freedoms, 63, 69

Postmaterialism, 49

Poverty: and capitalism, 2; and democracy, 4; and fundamentalism, 145; and the human-deprivation index, 63–64; and human needs, 5–7, 48–49; and infrastructures, 58–61, 62; and material goods, 1–3; rates of, 65, 67; shame of wealth amid, 58; three ideas in the idea of, 5. *See also* Human Development Index (HDI); Poor persons; Wealth

Pragmatism and environmentalism, 126

Prices: and demand, 34; and income, 37–38

Primitive cultures: affluence in, 3–4; contradictory lessons from, 167; ideas of the person in, 9,

11–14; transaction costs in, 167–169. *See also* Human Development Index (HDI); Social practice
Private property, evolution towards, 157, 167
Privatism, civic, 115–116
Production process, cultural, 69–72, 94
Profit, 35, 124
Progress and deprivation balance sheet, HDI: of developing countries, 64, 65–66; of industrial countries, 64, 66–68
Property rights, 157–158, 167
Prosperity and depression, cultural audit of, 138–139
Psychic needs, consumer, 39–40
Psychological economics, 41
Psychology: of anomie, 159; of ego multiplied by four, 106–109, 109 (fig.); folk, 83; or market theory, 44; and objectivity, 82–83, 107; sameness-of-individuals bias of, 51–52
Psychometry, 175–176
Public administration control models, 176–180
Public policy process, the: access of voices to, 124–125, 131; and argumentation processes, 125–126; and bounded rationality, 120–122; and civic responsiveness, 130–134; and the cultural-argument system, 125–128; cultural bias in, 122–125; cultural conflict over, 104, 105–106, 117–120, 185; and decision making, 150–152, 172–173; discourse coalitions in, 126–128;

exclusion from, 115–116; and irreconcilable conflicts, 128–130; monocultural or multicultural, 133; and sectarian violence, 119–120; as self-organizing, 128–129. *See also* Democracy; Justice; Politics
Punishment, 108, 168; expulsion as, 146, 179
Purchasing power, personal (PPP), GDP, 63, 64
Putnam, Robert, 130, 131–132

Quality of life and culture, 49–52. *See also* Communication needs; Needs, human; Wants

Raikes, Philip, 2
Random events, 170–171, 176
Randomness, contrived, 177–178
Rational choice: in animal societies, 87–88; as bounded, 120–122; and economic man, 44–45, 78–79, 129, 164–165, 175–176; and individualism, 103, 122. *See also* Consumer behavior; Public policy process, the
Rationalities, plural, 104
Rationality: bounded, 120–122; and decision making, 151–152; emotions as deviation from, 80–84; and human behavior, 75–77, 155; universality of logic and, 77–80. *See also* Objectivity
Rawls, John, 81
Rayner, Steve, 102, 147
Reciprocity, goods and social, 53
Redclift, Michael, 2
Relativism: totalizing, 19; of wealth, 100, 112

Religions: explanations of sects and, 85–86, 118, 142–145; and fundamentalism, 142–145, 152; and rationality, 75; the Sacred Book and decision making in, 150–151. *See also* Enclave culture

Replicators. *See* Memes

Research and cultural bias: international, 140n1, 142–145; of researchers, 17–18, 19

Resentment, 81

Returns, increasing, 170, 171

Ricardo, David, 5, 33, 35

Richards, Paul, 119, 134

Riesman, David, 161

Righteousness, and cultural bias, 117–120, 137–138. *See also* Enclave culture

Rights: human, 63; property, 157–158, 167; women's, 66, 67

Risk perception: cultural audits of, 138–141; as a cultural conflict forum, 135–138; and cultural theory, 136–138; and emotions, 84–85; as litmus test for cultural bias, 140–141; and moral hazards, 169; and saying nothing, 175–176; and wealth, 34

Roscher, Wilhelm Georg, 155

Rose-Ackerman, Susan, 178

Routinization, 158, 161

Rowntree Foundation, 116

Rural areas, 66; religious sects as from, 86

Sahlins, Marshall, 3, 4

Samuels, Warren J., 158

San Francisco Bay Area attitudes survey, 139–140

Satiability, the law of, 34–35, 39; economic, 39

Scale: of institutions, 146, 162, 167–169; of societies, 166–169

Schmoller, Gustav von, 155

Schmutzer, Manfred, 102, 183

Schwartz, B. I., 179

Science, social. *See* Social sciences

Science, tool-to-theory heuristic of, 29–33, 72, 74

Scott, W., 49–50

Seckler, D., 158

Sects: dissenting minorities and religious, 85–86, 118, 142–145; exclusivity of, 146–147; as youth movements, 152–153. *See also* Enclave culture

Security: in institutions, 169, 182; of the person, 50; of property rights, 157–158

Self-actualization needs, 51–52

Self-interest: and conscience, 155; individual competitive, 80, 122, 164–165

Selfishness, of replicators, 26–27

Self-regulating mechanisms, 36–38

Self-reproduction: and cultural bias, 123–124; and feedback, 31

Selle, Per, 140n1

Sen, Amartya, 52, 58–61, 62, 70, 72

Shelter indicators, 50, 66

Simplicity: and poverty, 3–4; and smallness of scale, 167–168

Sivan, Emmanuel, 120, 150–151, 152

Size of societies, 4, 166–169

Slither theory: of enclave development, 147–149, 172; of institutional evolution, 172–173

Small-is-beautiful concept, 4, 167–168

Social beings: cultural feedback cycle of, 31, 91–92, 93, 123–124, 163; negative freedoms of, 69–72; and nonhuman intelligence, 86–88; theories of, 46–47. *See also* Person, theory of the whole

Social capital, 69, 72, 130

Social constructs, definition of, 126

Social policy studies. *See* Policy sciences

Social practice: among primates, 87–88; and economic disruption, 138–139, 144–145; and the history of ideas, 29, 96; poverty and infrastructures of, 58–61; progress and deprivation, 65–68, 144–145. *See also* Primitive cultures

Social sciences: comparisons between the, 9, 48–49, 156–157; cultural bias in the, 51–52, 157–162, 179, 182, 184; hostility to intellectualist, 12; integrating the, 96, 163; political analysis avoided by, 94, 129; self as nonsocial in, 5–7, 8, 89, 184; studying institutions, 154. *See also* Economic theory; *specific science or theory names*

Social security: indicators, 67; risk perceptions, 138–139

Social theories: avoiding context-independent, 108; embedded in economic practices and institutions, 30; and family organization, 110–112, 111 (fig.); and globalization, 15–16, 19; and social theory about acceptability of, 21, 96

Social theory of the person. *See* Person, theory of the whole

Sociology: cultural bias in, 161–162; of institutions, 156, 158–162; religious, 85–86; role theory, 160

Spencer, Herbert, 157, 167

Spiritual needs, 47. *See also* Religions

Standard of living: Human Development Index (HDI) of, 61–69; Level of Living Index of, 49–51

Starvation, 58–61, 68

Status, importance of. *See* Hierarchy, the culture of

Stereotyping: in cultural opposition, 123–124; of institutions, 162, 177

Strathern, Marilyn, 8, 93

Subsistence, need for measures of, 5, 6–7, 8, 17

Suicide and anomie, 159

Surplus income. *See* Income

Surveys: of attitudes toward technology, 139–140; consumer confidence, 41; Human Development Index (HDI), 61, 62–69

Survival: of institutions, 180–183; measures of human, 5, 6–7, 65–68

Swedlow, Brendan, 127

Szasz, Thomas, 128

Tastes, communication through, 53–58, 55 (fig.), 57 (fig.)

Taylor, Michael, 167–168

Technologies: adoption of, 170; communication, 68, 73, 182–183; cultural audits of attitudes toward, 139–140, 140n1;

Technologies *(continued)*
and institutional control strategies, 180–183; and institutions,
158; nuclear, 129–130, 140; and
path dependence, 170–171; and
social isolation, 115–116. *See also*
Environmentalism; Industrial
world, the
Teleology, avoiding, 26–27
Terrorist groups, sectarian,
119–120
Theory of culture. *See* Cultural
theory
The Theory of Political Economy
(Jevons), 34
Thévenot, Laurent, 21, 97, 99,
100, 182
Things and goods: circulation of,
53–54; communication through
tastes in, 53–58, 55 (fig.), 57
(fig.); expenditure items, 42n1;
and poverty, 1–3; private and
public, 62, 167–169; as symbolic, 47, 53–58
Thompson, Michael, 101–102,
104, 110–111, 115, 138
Time structure: and household
culture, 109–112, 111 (fig.); and
standard of living, 49
Tools-to-theory heuristic, the, 29–
33; *Homo œconomicus* as exemplifying, 74; in international comparisons, 72
Transaction costs, 165–166; in
primitive societies, 168–169
Turnbull, Colin, 3
Turner, Brian, 161
Tversky, Amos, 77–78

Unemployment, 67; as voluntary,
37

United Nations Human Development Index (HDI), 61, 62–63,
68–69; balance sheet, 65–68;
human-deprivation index,
HDIs, 63–64
United Nations Research Institute for Social Development
(UNRISD), 49–50
Universality: of logic and rationality, 77–80; of pluralism, 121–122
Universe, microcosm as macrocosm of the, 24–25, 31–32
Universities, peer review in, 178,
180
Urban areas: progress and deprivation in, 66; risk perception in,
139–140; road planning policies
in, 133
Utility theory: about wants not
needs, 43; dependence on physiology model, 40–43; and Engel's
Law, 42–43; growth into microcosm, 36–38; marginal returns
theory applied to, 33–36; microcosmic levels of, 39–40, 182–
183; the person in, 163–164,
183–184; and rationality, 75–80,
120. *See also* Economic theory;
Rational choice

Values: focus on the individual's,
76–77; hierarchy of, 48–49; and
organizational purposes, 103,
122–123, 163–165; research
based on competing, 107–108.
See also Cultural bias
Varian, Hal R., 81
Veblen, Thorstein, 158
Village life, loss of, 144–145
Violence: against women, 67; sectarian, 119–120, 147

Virtues, civic norms or, 130–131
Voices, cultural. *See* Public policy process, the
Vulgarity and taste, 54, 55 (fig.), 56

Wages, 67, 78–79
Wagner, Peter, 160, 161
Walras, Léon, 34
Wants, theories of: and basic cultural needs, 49–52; and conscience, 155; or market theory, 42–43, 44, 95; and tastes, 53–58. *See also* Needs, human
Wars and conflicts: civil, 117, 119–120; and fundamentalism, 143, 146, 152
Wealth: and altruism, 9, 48–49, 93; cultural theory not based on relative, 100, 112; exclusion from, 116, 148; and fundamentalism, 144–145; poverty as converse of, 1–2; and risk, 34; and standard of living, 49–51, 61–69. *See also* Poverty
Weber, Max, 89, 160
Wedding presents, and taste: contemporary, 56–58, 57 (fig.); Victorian, 54, 55 (fig.), 56
Weiss, C. Hirschon, 161
Welfare: components and indicators of, 49–51; in the context of policy, 6–8; cost of, 182; and poverty theory, 4. *See also* Public policy process, the
Well-being: four cultural attitudes toward, 122–123; individualist conception of, 121–122; international comparisons of, 61–69; and social mechanisms of allocation, 71–72

Western civilization: and European national histories, 16–17; fragility of industrial democracy and, 14–17; industrial countries in, 66–68; theory of the person in, 10–11. *See also* Technologies
Whaling controversy, 130
Whitley, R., 161
Whole persons. *See* Person, theory of the whole
Wildavsky, Aaron, 104, 139, 175, 179, 181–182
Wilder, Thornton, 98–99, 100, 112–113
Williamson, Oliver E., 120, 166
Winter, Sydney, 164
Wittgenstein, Ludwig, 12
Wittrock, B., 161
Wollman, H., 161
Women: as isolates, 113–114; progress and deprivation of, 66, 67
Woodburn, James, 3
World religions. *See* Religions
Worlds: cultural bias and plural, 97–100, 104–106; of developing and industrial countries, 65–68; ego and personality types in four, 106–109, 139–140; selecting the number of, 100–102. *See also* Cultural types, the four

Xenophobia, 84–86

Younghusband, Francis, 28
Youth movements, 152–153

Zealotry. Enclave culture

Text: 10/15 Janson
Display: Janson
Compositor, Printer, and Binder: Braun-Brumfield, Inc.